The Winter is Past

Helen Weston was born in Lancashire in 1949 and studied English at St Hilda's College, Oxford. After a variety of jobs, she joined a religious community at the age of 26 and stayed there for five years.

THE WINTER IS PAST

HELEN WESTON

For Hilary

With many thanks for your
hospitality and humour
Love — Helen (Weston)

TRIANGLE

First published in Great Britain in 1995
Triangle Books
Society for Promoting Christian Knowledge
Holy Trinity Church
Marylebone Road
London NW1 4DU

The author and publisher would like to thank the following for
permission to reproduce copyright material:

Fowler-Wright Books for the extract from *The Second Journey: Spiritual
Awareness and the Mid-Life Crisis* by Gerald O'Collins on pages 85–6. This
book was first published by the Paulist Press in 1978. New edition to be
published by Gracewing in 1995.

Penguin Books for the extract from *Ring of Bright Water* by Gavin
Maxwell, on page 38. This book was first published in 1960.

Oxford University Press for the extract from 'Now the Green Blade
Riseth' on page 168. Words by J.M.C. Crum, reproduced from the
Oxford Book of Carols
© 1928 Oxford University Press.

Orion Publishing Group Ltd for the extract from 'The Initials in the
Heart' by Laurence Whistler on page 72. This book was first published
by Rupert Hart-Davis in 1964.

British Library Cataloguing-in-Publication Data
A catalogue record for this book is available from the British Library

ISBN 0–281–04854–1

Typeset by Dorwyn Ltd, Rowlands Castle, Hants
Printed and bound in Great Britain by
BPC Paperbacks Ltd
Member of the British Printing Company Ltd

Contents

To my mother

My special thanks are due to Helen Reed, whose enthusiasm pushed me into writing this story, Sue Mayo, whose expertise helped me get started on it and Christine Bicknell, who heroically coped with the typing of it.

1
Pas de Deux

It was seven years before it was possible even to think about writing this book. The two years it took to write were painful years because the process brought back so much that was fragmented and unresolved. But since we have moved into the cathedral close at Carlisle, and back into a daily rhythm of shared life and worship, there has come an unexpected sense of healing.

What had once seemed merely an exodus now begins to look like part of a more complex redemptive pattern; and it seems possible, at last, to integrate the monastic experience into our everyday lives. Because of this new sense of pattern and cohesion, it is easier to share what is an intensely personal story. Perhaps it may be a help for others struggling with comparable moral dilemmas.

Our sons, Luke and Alexander, are now nine and five respectively. Fifteen years ago I was on the verge of taking final vows in an Anglican convent, full of a sense of loss that I would never have children of my own. I was 31 years old and time was running out.

Their father was the 43 year old abbot of an Anglican Benedictine monastery, and we had yet to meet.

The story of how we crossed the physical and emotional space between us and came together is what this book is about.

I have begun with myself because, although this is a story told by two voices, mine is the narrative voice; David's is filtered through his letters and poems. Consequently, the bias is also mine. This was a conscious decision by both of us – partly for practical reasons, and partly for aesthetic ones.

The story begins in October 1980, shortly after my thirty-first birthday. My name in community was Sister Helen Simon. David's was Dom Wilfrid.

I was the first novice for ten years to have got so close to making a life commitment in the Society of All Saints, Oxford, and I felt trapped. I was trapped both by the expectations of the community and by the promises I had made to God at my temporary vows nearly three years previously.

There was also a dimension which was possibly masochistic, possibly a result of my upbringing, maybe even a peculiarly female anxiety, namely that I had no right to seek my own selfish happiness while other people were suffering – there seemed to be an endless supply of suffering people.

I remember the sense of being locked into tramlines that led nowhere except to old age and death; deviations were not possible. I remember recurring dreams of escape, full of run-away cars and free flight and murdering people; but I had no 'inner permission' to go.

Well-meaning priests told me that I should learn to grieve for the lost children I would never have, but instead I wrote poems:

> The child-want is so deep an ache
> That one day there will come a crack
> Like rock that earthquake shook
> Along the fault-line;
> And when they come with instruments
> To probe and look
> They will find me neatly halved
> And perfect in each stony bed
> A fossil foetus carved.

While all this struggle was going on I met Dom Wilfrid Weston, abbot of Nashdom Abbey, in Buckinghamshire, and slowly everything began to shift. We met at Vauxhall in south London, as members of a team of men and women (lay, clerical and religious) who were living together for a week as part of an experiment in community living.

We had renovated a derelict vicarage and disused church, and had arranged all sorts of group activities, exhibitions and discussions as part of our interaction with the local parish. The idea was to see if some of the insights and strengths of community living could be a resource for churches in deprived urban settings. The initiative was a joint venture of the local priest and one of the Benedictine monks, as part of the celebrations for the 1,500th anniversary of St Benedict's birth.

Although Dom Wilfrid was the abbot, he was at Vauxhall simply as one of the team; he was not in charge – though it was difficult at first to remember that. He and I were allocated the job of hanging some rather makeshift home-made curtains at the vast empty windows of the vicarage. An advance party had already made the place habitable, and done some basic decorating.

He seemed like the perfect monk in bearing and appearance. His face was austerely beautiful, with only a glimmer of sensuality about the lips. In his black Benedictine habit and hooded scapular, he looked a quintessentially medieval figure, from a world of cloisters and shadows and haunting plainsong. But in his jeans and denim shirt he was simply a strong, rather spare man in his early forties, with a marked reserve about him.

I was rather put off by his austerity and seniority, and wished I had been paired with one of the younger, more extrovert characters. But as the week progressed something deep in me was stirred by his response to the warmth of those around him. It was as if he had never experienced *real* community before; affection and tenderness seemed to be completely new discoveries to him, and it was poignant to watch him gravely sharing these discoveries in our group discussions.

When I stood next to him in the services in chapel, which we put together ourselves, there was an almost unbearable sweetness in sharing a book with him, or accidentally touching his hand. Nothing was said, of course, but there was a complicated expression in his eyes one morning when he saw me without my veil, drying my hair. I couldn't be sure that it was any more than the affection that was springing up between us all, but for a moment his face was unguarded, and he really looked at me, with something like desire or longing in his eyes.

In 'normal' circumstances such thoughts would have been ludicrous – junior sisters did not even initiate conversations with superiors, much less cherish feelings of affection (or love?) for them. And yet I thought I caught him out in small acts of special tenderness – such as allocating me an extra quilt for my bed, or engineering a visit to a local Orthodox monastery for the two of us alone. But I had very little to go on. Possibly his final hug, as he embraced us all in farewell, was a little more passionate for me than the others, but I wasn't sure.

One conversation does stand out, though, in the kitchen quite late at night, as I remember. Ostensibly I was asking his advice about whether or not I should leave my own community (which I had more or less decided to do), but the conversation quickly got on to his own situation, which he used as an illustration of what would happen to me if I stayed. The image he used to describe his own state within the monastery was of being 'deep frozen'. He spoke of the advantages of having one's feelings so numbed, but the main impression was one of resignation. The important thing, he said, was to hand on the tradition intact to the next generation.

I was appalled, and argued with him passionately that this could hardly be a valid expression of the love of Christ, but I was aware of not making much headway. Luckily, I was able to let off steam to my room-mate, Sue Mayo, who was one of the instigators of the project, and somehow knew intuitively what I was feeling. She was like a bright 'alter ego' for me: living out in her life many of the things I would love to have done and hadn't dared to – such as street theatre and dance. But in her way, she was also a deeply disturbing presence, beckoning me out of community to a richer life on the outside.

When I got back to my own community in the heart of the West End, there was no opportunity to unwind, as the sister-in-charge was going away and the other sisters had already had to cover for me for a week. It was back to work – cleaning rooms and serving meals in the students' hostel we ran – knowing that the ideals of the week meant a rededication to community life, when the sense of loss was overwhelming.

I remember trying to get the tears over before we went into lunch, because it wasn't done to draw attention to oneself during silent meals, and it was so silent compared with Vauxhall. It was the inexorability of it all that was the most painful thing. He would go back to his 'deep-freeze' and I to my treadmill, and we'd struggle to be noble and forbearing and faithful, when all we wanted (or at least I wanted) was some chance to explore this new quickening. Perhaps it was stillborn already. The thought of it all made me feel unutterably weary.

But then a letter arrived. It was a baffling mixture of fatherly and personal reactions. It ended with something like an abbatial blessing, yet it began with talk of alchemy, hinting at a personal experience of fire: 'Rather the base metal of my heart glowed briefly to reflect a warmth and richness not its own.'

4

And it referred, surely, to our experience of working alongside each other hanging those curtains?

> Always my understanding lagged behind events
> Our common tasks were done
> Before our adjacent hands had learnt to touch
> And know the threshold of a new communion.

Yet there was nothing tangible, nothing there one could rely on, and events were beginning to move fast within my own community. I pushed down my feelings, keeping them for the privacy of my cell, where I could take them out and hug them to myself. I kept the letter always with me, in the deep pocket of my habit.

There was to be a reunion of the community project in December which I had gained permission to attend. In the meantime I was struggling with the issue of whether or not I should remain in community. My instincts were all for leaving. Bodily symptoms such as headaches, vertigo and backache reinforced this. But an awful inner conviction was growing that I had to remain celibate: I couldn't leave and get married and have children and be happy in a 'normal' way, because what I loved more than anything was the beauty of suffering and heroic self-sacrifice.

The evidence seemed to be piling up against me. The message of our retreat had been about sacrificial loving, and a recent sermon from a much-loved priest had said the same thing. Even my dreams were reinforcing the message; a particularly vivid one had warned that marriage would remove 'the bloody heart' of me, like some form of sterilization.

I also struggled with the knowledge that the beauty of the community life at Vauxhall, though it came from the participation of flesh-and-blood people, was about this same self-sacrifice. With Wilfrid himself, the loveliness lay in his dedication. Even if one visualized tearing him away from it, it would kill him and ultimately the love itself.

It was a bleak thought that I had to let my deepest longings wither in order to give him space to be. I longed just to touch his face, I was convinced that my love and tenderness could bring something to birth in him that would complete him, yet I knew it had to happen in the spiritual realm and not the physical. I thrashed about inside, trying to avoid the knowledge that the only motherhood I could hope for would be spiritual.

But still I didn't want to accept it. I knew that something in Wilfrid had stirred the feminine in me with such force that I couldn't afford to let it die again. I didn't *want* to sublimate it or transmute it: I wanted to live it out. Psychotherapy over the previous year of struggles had taught me of the deep need to 'inhabit the feminine' in myself. I had begun to recognize that my religious vocation had come from the tomboy in me, who had always wanted to be a knight of the Round Table, a crusader. I had always identified with the hero, not the heroine, but it was slowly killing me. In many of my dreams over the last few months, the feminine part of myself seemed to be forcing itself into my consciousness. Loving and responding as a woman I knew was the answer, but I also knew that I could hope for nothing from Dom Wilfrid as he had his own burdens to bear.

Nevertheless, I went to the reunion on 13 December and I saw him across a crowded room; a crowded room full of people who must suspect nothing – and, indeed, who must have nothing to suspect. But as he turned to look at me his eyes burned for a second, and I do not know what my own hopelessly expressive face showed. The two days of the reunion were painful, as I was in no state myself to make plans for the future of the Vauxhall community. I felt intensely vulnerable – both from my hidden love for Dom Wilfrid and my turmoil about leaving my own community. He, on the other hand, seemed absorbed and happy, talking companionably with a female religious who was assisting him with detailed plans for the next stage. I was jealous, and felt an outsider.

One event again stands out. We came to the last sermon for our farewell service. It looked as if Wilfrid would have to write it as he was the senior priest, and was used to producing homilies at the drop of a hat. We all knew that this went against the spirit of our equal sharing of tasks, but nobody offered to take it on. Suddenly I heard myself offer to do it, even though I didn't have the remotest idea what I was going to say. In the event, Dom Wilfrid and I went into different rooms, agreeing that whoever came up with a sermon first would preach it.

I finished first, as the sermon seemed to deliver itself on to the page with hardly a thought on my part. I cannot remember much about it except that I tried to convey some of the expectation of Advent – as it then was – from a woman's point of view. I must have talked about pregnancy, about bearing the Christ-child. Something about things growing in darkness, about soil and concrete, about tenderness and strength, must have been uppermost, because the images started off a chain reaction in Wilfrid that had repercussions for years afterwards. His letter to me on 19 December 1980 had this to say:

19 December 1980

Your sermon on Sunday seemed to say it all. I believe that you do have both the necessary insights and the necessary gifts to break up the concrete, to bring in the soil, to plant the seeds, and to nurture the plants which will make the wilderness blossom . . . I cannot believe that you have to reconcile yourself to a situation where these gifts cannot be exercised.

He seemed to be saying here and elsewhere in the letter that the religious life was too constricting a place for me, though for himself he was reconciled to it. But my search for a more passionate commitment from him towards me was hard to sustain in the face of his measured affectionate words.

So it was back to my own battle in the community. My will to remain was stretched to breaking point, but it had not yet snapped. I had been sent to the London House from the Mother House in Oxford a year previously because I had been proving too much of a thorn in their flesh. I knew that my rebelliousness was partly due to my own hang-up about authority. A basic tenet of the vow of obedience was that one obeyed a superior without question, as a representative of God; love or respect for that person did not enter into it. I had never been able to do this.

It had been all right while I was a novice because I had worshipped my novice-mistress, Sister Frances Dominica, so that everything she asked me to do was invested not only with love, but an aura of sanctity. I had been cocooned by my love and respect for her, and had not yet come up against the harsh realities of community life: the boredom, the jealousies and the loneliness.

However, when I took my first vows, I was pushed out of the nest, and she was also elected head of the community, becoming Mother Frances (Dominica). From a state of almost symbiotic union, I became just one of her 'flock', and was left to fend for myself. Several of the sisters made a special attempt to befriend me, but it wasn't enough. Without the transfusion of her love and idealism, community was an arid place.

I also knew too much. I had seen at first hand the risks she took with relationships, her radical bending of the rules. I could square it all with the Rule when I was her trusted confidante, but when she pulled away from me and admonished me to pull myself together, live the life more rigorously, it was like an echo of adolescence – 'don't do as I do, do as I say' – and it brought out all my rebelliousness. She was often absent from chapel or meals in the refectory – both fundamental duties of a religious – and I grew bitter as she criticized me for going off the rails, when her example had led me there. Yet to the community she was a beacon of love and purity – and, still was for me, despite all, which made it worse.

I was banished to London, overwhelmed by my own weakness and failure, yet conscious that some subtle abuse of power was going on which I could not unmask out of loyalty to her. It was January 1980, some nine months before the Vauxhall project, and I had just begun having psychotherapy once a week (in Oxford!) with a therapist called Wendy Robinson. The psychotherapy was deemed necessary because of my inability to fit into the system, and because of my own personal unhappiness.

2

Breaking Out

My time in the London House started off well, as the sister-in-charge shared many of my intellectual interests, and was cool enough to give my bruised feelings time to mend. But jealousies emerged here too, and basic differences of interpretation of the Rule and the vows. In retrospect, I can see that I was the start of a new wave of novices who unwittingly brought the forces of change and renewal to the Community; but at the time it was an unpleasant and bewildering experience to be so at odds with the system.

As the sociologist Goffman has pointed out, the religious life has many of the properties of a 'total institution', in much the same way as a prison or an asylum. What that means in practice is that there is no relief from the glare, no place to go and shut the door; you are on parade 24 hours a day in a convent. There can be no subversive sub-culture if you are to live the life wholeheartedly.

The sister-in-charge in London, Sister H, was a cultured person with a great belief in justice and reason and talking things out. I was impulsive, intense. My great need was for openness, hers was for privacy or perhaps discretion. We began to clash. She felt I overstepped the bounds in my relations with the students. I felt I was only being human. She had the power; and as she retrenched, I became more and more boxed in.

I was reprimanded almost daily for breaches of discipline, so that I grew clumsy and began to make even more mistakes. I grew tense and defiant. I was supposed to be in charge of the domestic side of the house. My cleaning was deficient, my duty rosters were not up to date, and my time-keeping was abominable. I always left the lights on, I talked unnecessarily in silence times. I found occasion for too many outside engagements. All this was publicly itemized to the other sisters at morning 'Obediences', where notices and duties for the day were handed out.

'Obediences' had started out informally (unlike in the Mother House), and was conducted with affection, but over my year at the House it had grown into a battleground. Part of me was profoundly sorry, as I had great respect for the sister-in-charge, but by November/December of 1980 we were on a collision course, which somehow could not be altered, despite our attempts at reconciliation.

My journal entry for that period illustrates the situation:

22 November 1980 – Journal Entry

Lurching from one clash to another. Yesterday was the meeting about coffee consumption, and how *some of us* were extravagant. Today it was the fact that I hadn't mentioned A's arrival which upset the portressing rota. Also I was correcting my sermon at dinner, which got a public reprimand – unheard of at silent meals. I was full of dumb insolence outwardly and murderous rage inside. Totally unable to give an inch – to apologize or explain.

Felt like a cow or some other obstinate beast, who's been brought to the end of her rope and digs her heels in. Even more like a dog who is beaten just so much and then turns round and snarls.

Was like that when Sister H asked me to 'explain' my behaviour. At first I just said nothing at all as she gave me her 'rational' explanation of the inconsistency, plain bad manners (that hurt) and disobedience, of my behaviour. I couldn't hear her properly – it was like I saw stars or blood – and her arguments were like bits of alien twisted metal that didn't fit any approach to life that I knew.

Finally I just broke through and I said I was totally beyond any rational behaviour. Her belief that my behaviour was a deliberate, provocative 'ploy' was so way off the mark that I had to tell her. Said I was totally twisted up emotionally and just felt I could murder her; that community standards and all the rest of it were completely beyond me now. I kept shuddering and crying uncontrollably.

And she got gentler and gentler, like she was talking to someone dangerously ill. But genuinely kind in the end: came and stood with her arms round me and somehow we got to the point that it really was best to leave. That no failure – that it hurt so much more for her to see me like that.

Also I saw what my behaviour was doing to her – totally out of control – wreaking havoc, like a driverless car. No longer a question of will driving emotions – emotions broken free. . . . Gradually we talked of practicalities . . .

I agreed to try and stick it out until my vows were up – October 1981. We had even made plans to try and work together on some areas of the Rule that needed re-thinking. But it was not good – even with the pressure off we continued to short circuit each other and the atmosphere between us was like an electrical storm. I felt physically afraid – both of her anger and my own. There was also a spiritual fear, which was even worse.

8 January 1981 – Journal Entry

Underneath all this constant battling is a quiet, crumbling fear, like cliff erosion, that I am denying God something, that the choice of leaving is evading an obedience issue which is crucial to any integrity I have left.

I was feverishly trying to finish reading Monica Furlong's biography of Thomas Merton, racing against my own imminent dissolution, hoping against hope that I would somehow find an answer to my questions about vocation and obedience. There was some sort of answer when Merton finally came to the conclusion that his primary vocation was to be a man, and after that a writer, and only then – 'to facilitate the other two' – a monk.

But by then there had been another explosive confrontation between the sister-in-charge and myself, and it was too late. I had exploded in public, said the unsayable, shocked the most holy of the senior sisters, and there was no going back – on either side. The decision had been made for me: I was out – sent to a half-way house in Oxford, to cool my heels and think things out.

Dom Wilfrid was ignorant of most of this turmoil. I must have written to him, attempting to explain my current situation, because there is a letter from him dated 3 February 1981, responding to my letter. It was sent to the London House, but by then I had already been whisked away 'in a closed van'.

I spent the first night in the Mother House at Oxford, but as far as the sisters were concerned, I arrived under cover of darkness and was dispatched in the same way. I encountered some affection, but mostly embarrassment – or the sort of fear you inspire when you are infectious.

That night – in my room in the hostel (I wasn't invited to sleep in the sisters' house) – I experienced my own private absolution, which made the whole exodus possible. It was simply a tangible sense that God had come in the closed van with me, and was not left behind ('I was hooded but always with you'). Merton was right: vocation was about finding your own deepest truth and staying loyal to it. At last I could sleep.

Dom Wilfrid's letter – read in the first days spent in my half-way house – (a neighbouring religious community) – was like balm. He apologized for the 'facile' comments in his last letter, which had assumed I would emerge from community like a butterfly from a chrysalis, without pain or regret; but he reiterated that he was glad I would probably leave the religious life.

Still deploying the imagery of that Vauxhall sermon, he explained what he had tried to say in the previous letter:

3 February 1981

> It is very evident to me that the concrete needs the soil. Concrete in this context seemed to mean not only Vauxhall's urban squalor, but the life-denying institutionalism of Religious life.
>
> My hope for you had been that you would leave the 'concrete' world and explore a world where 'soil' was the natural element. Identifying myself with the concrete, I did not want selfishly to hold on to you . . .

He then addressed himself to a possibility that had obviously never occurred to him before: 'Can soil need the concrete? It is this question that your letter seems particularly to raise in my mind. Is the unselfishness of letting go the ultimate selfishness?'

At last there was a chink in the armour. I replied by return – but then rescued my passionate response from the outgoing mail before it was collected! My second, more measured, letter (of which I kept a copy) seems hardly less passionate.

My dear – I want to say so much but I hardly dare – written words carry such resonance and power, as you know only too well. Suffice it to say that soil has *great need* of concrete, and this soil more than most. But some concrete is no thicker than the last layer of ice in the spring as it melts from underneath, and what emerges is very vulnerable with great need of cherishing, but with phenomenal potential for growth and beauty . . .

In this and subsequent letters over the next three months, we tried to arrange a meeting, and even in my subdued state, the cloak-and-dagger aspect of it appealed to both my romantic and subversive sides.

It felt wrong to be in another convent when I knew I had burst those bonds. Despite the nuns' kindness, I felt irked by the 30 watt light bulbs in the corridors, the ten-minute restriction on bath times, the necessity to learn a whole new system of rules and customs just in order to survive. I felt as if the prioress was trying to retrieve my vocation, when my real need was to be with people who could help me practically – to find a job and a place to live.

However, they were very good about giving me time to myself and space to work things out. I worked in the garden and the kitchen and I shared their (silent) meals, but apart from attending chapel there were no other community obligations. There were privileges too. I wasn't required to get up for the night-time office, and every evening before bed I was presented with a thermos of hot chocolate. I combined the drink with some Liquorice Allsorts I had been given in London, which I rationed out to one a day! It felt like feverish self-indulgence, but I felt I had to practise. It was the same with novels – reading them was like secret drinking. I read *The Towers of Trebizond* and *Testament of Youth* in quick succession, particularly relishing Rose Macaulay's wit and irony after five years of earnest self-improvement.

Yet there was much inner work to do. I read all the notes and diaries I had kept since the novitiate, and struggled to come to terms with the sense of failure and waste and loss –

and the anger too. It was like divorce, or bereavement. I kept circling round and round the same questions: Could I have behaved any differently? Should I have stayed? It was as if my instincts had made the decision, and my will had to catch up.

Throughout this month I went twice a week for psychotherapy with Wendy, without whose love and support I could hardly have attempted the necessary reconstruction work. Other friends, as well as Wendy, were rallying round – many of them with offers of practical help – though my access to them was limited. I went to see my family only once, because I felt I had to make it on my own as an adult, and the desire to succumb to their love and sympathy was too strong when I was there. I was 31 after all, even if I did feel like a lost child.

On 12 February 1981 I received another letter from Wilfrid. He had written immediately assuring me of his 'love and caring' and 'a sort of wondering unknowing that enhances both'. Before my reply reached him, he wrote again, charged with the need to communicate to me his discovery of 'tenderness'. To me it seemed a restatement of something I had witnessed in him at Vauxhall, but it came to him as a 'revelation' after reading Neville-Ward's *The Following Plough*:

12 February 1981

> I wonder if you can find a copy of this book. . . . Certainly, for me, the book has enabled me to see that 'your' word tenderness sums up much that had been closed to me in the area of thoughts and feelings. But, without you it would have been just another paragraph in just another book. Because you had made me aware of this enigma within me, I read the book from a new standpoint, and recognized in the word 'tenderness' a quality not just appropriate for others, but something with which I needed to come to terms. What the implications of this discovery may be I have yet to learn . . .

A postscript to the letter was another poem he had written, inspired by a quotation from Balzac:

> Last issued from the hands that shaped the world
> she, the purest expression of God's thought,

is not, like man, torn from primordial rock
formed by God's fingers from the dust of earth.
No, she is drawn from the tender substance of man's side,
bone of Adam's bone, flesh of his flesh;
He who had not help fit for him
receives, from God's hand, she whom He had wonderfully
made.

In response, I sent him one of my most treasured possessions: a small card that showed a rough clay sculpture of a tiny
baby held in the palms of two hands. It reminded him of Psalm
139 (a psalm that had also been a great favourite of mine),
which he quoted in his next letter:

> You have searched me out and known me
> and covered me with your hand.
> You have made me and fashioned me
> and formed my inward parts.
> It was your eyes that saw my body
> while it was yet imperfect
> when I was made in secret
> and woven in the depths of the earth . . .

There was another poem too, beginning with these words:

> Your word comes as the sweet life-giving dew
> which softens the brittle, dry and hardened clay
> to be refashioned by the potter's hand
> and bear the impress of love's fingerprint.

It seemed a strange irony even then that while my love was
clearly quickening new life in Wilfrid, my own strength was
ebbing away. I remember sitting at my desk looking out over
the garden, which looked utterly bare and lifeless, and envy-
ing a fly that crawled across my window with such apparent
purpose. I felt as if the last five years had just been a frantic
attempt to impose meaning and structure on a life that was
totally empty of meaning, and all the structures were now
flattened.

Perversely, that rock-bottom state was the moment when
things began to mend. I wrote in my journal:

13 February 1981 – Journal Entry

There are still, even at rock bottom, microscopic things that give the lie to the meaninglessness. I must work with these tiny things – almost like brick-dust – and build meaning *right* from the bottom. It must be my own building – so that I can rely on it – and nothing big must be used in it, nothing I can't be sure of, like Wilfrid's love, or a satisfying career, or even my own writing. It must be a belief in *life* for bare *life*'s sake.

What do I actually *want* at this moment? Space, trees, hills, the sea – a place of my own, music. Coffee, of course. There are a few crucial books, my prayer-stool, two or three beautiful objects (like my bloodstone ring, the tortoiseshell vase, the reindeer skin). And some sort of car, so that I can be independent . . .

'Don't fence me in' was like a leitmotiv that ran through my days. Although I was so lonely, I wanted freedom far more than human company; it was almost like a physical thirst.

When Mother Frances came to see me for the first time, I was depressed by her apparent expectation that I would just collapse when I left community. She said something like, 'Oh, you won't go back just to what you were, will you?' She was bright and warm and sympathetic as usual, but underneath she expected me to fail. She promised some financial help, and I plucked up the courage to ask for some money to buy a second-hand car. She wasn't encouraging, though in the end the community did give me £500. (My mother later amused herself by calculating how much I was 'owed' for five years of round-the-clock work, including overtime and weekends!)

Wendy's visit a short time afterwards was so different. We talked about the 'brick-dust', and she said how important it was that when I left I had a base on which to stand – some sort of home of my own before returning to my family.

But where? An unexpected visit from my friend Philippa, who lived across the road from the Mother House in Oxford, and had shared many ups and downs with me, provided a solution. Her parents had a cottage in Suffolk, not far from Cambridge. She said I could have it rent-free, until I had worked out what I wanted to do. Then I had a phone call from another close friend, Rosemary, who had stuck with me from the days we had worked together at Oxfam head office, and braved the restrictions of convent visiting despite her own trepidation. She offered to pick me up from the Mother House the day I left, and to take me back to her flat, where I could stay as long as I liked.

Both of these practical demonstrations of caring were crucial life-lines for me, and could be accepted gratefully as they came from friends of my own age who were no threat to my autonomy.

My feelings for Wilfrid, on the other hand, were part of the old ache that was identified with the religious life. I knew that what I needed just then were down-to-earth expressions of affection – a chance to re-enter ordinary life, watch telly, drink lots of coffee, listen to ribald jokes, and just let go. In contrast, Wilfrid stood for discipline, self-sacrifice and intensity, and even though I responded to him from the depths of my soul, it was dangerous – it felt like regression. When I spoke to Wendy about my love for him in one of our psychotherapy sessions, I could see that she too had qualms, though she did no more than wonder out loud if he knew what he was asking for: was it really me he was responding to, or an ideal image of womanhood?

As the time for departure approached, the need grew 'to make a good end'. I wanted to do something about all the jagged bits, all the unresolved feelings and misunderstandings. I needed to make sense of my five tempestuous years in community, and give them a decent burial. But the day came with this need still unmet, although I saw Mother Frances several times during the preceding month.

It was snowing as I left one convent and walked with my suitcase to the other. I was almost late for the communion service and sat in the ante-chapel – already half out of the community. There were two shining new novices in choir, who had been 'clothed' only the night before. I felt like a fallen angel; yet no one noticed me much, as my arrival had not been officially announced – or my departure.

It was all so haphazard and painful – trying to say goodbye to people I had lived with for five years of my life, when two-thirds of them didn't even know I was leaving and the other third were embarrassed. I longed for some official rite of passage, some ceremony at which I could remove the habit and veil, the girdle, cross and ring with the same dignity as I had received them. Instead, I was told – doubtless with kind intentions – that I could pack them up in a cardboard box and bring them back when I had time.

There was a final talk with Mother Frances, in which I forced some honest confrontation of the love and the pain that had passed between us. And then it was all over. Rosemary drove me home. It was Sunday, 22 February 1981.

3

Points of Departure

Wilfrid and I had come to monastic life by very different routes. Born at opposite ends of the country, we were separated also by the experience of war. Wilfrid was born in Brighton in 1937, and I was born in Lancashire in 1949. My home town was St Helens, a town dominated by Pilkingtons Glass and Beechams Pills. There were pits encircling the town, and the smell of Greenall Whitley's breweries infused it. The market sold the best tripe for miles around, and there were still women who did their shopping in their curlers, and scrubbed and whitened their doorsteps – just as our relations down south thought they did.

I half belonged and half didn't, because my father was from Sussex and we inhabited two quite distinct worlds, depending on which set of relations we were with. I was ribbed for my accent wherever I was: in St Helens it was too posh, down south it was quaintly northern.

As I grew up I couldn't wait to get out and go somewhere exotic and beautiful, but I was also very happy there. I had several close friends, a lively, close-knit family – with my granny ten minutes' walk away – and I went to a school that I liked very much.

I often think of the stages of my life as symbolized by my two grannies. My mother's mother, whom we called 'Gangy', was fat, warm and bloody-minded – a sort of amalgam of the battling grandmother in the Giles cartoons and Laurie Lee's mother in *Cider with Rosie*! While she was with us in my childhood, turning out sherry trifles and Christmas puds, doing the ironing with her hat on, crying with laughter at graveyard jokes or dialect tales, I took her gritty, humorous outlook for granted. I loved her fiercely but always yearned after the culture and the glamour of the south.

My father's mother was a complete mental and physical contrast. She lived in Hastings, was slim and cool and bookish, and tended to offer us China tea while talking decorously about Beatrix Potter – whom she had once met when she was a governess in the Lake District. She was a representative of another world, which we visited once a year, in our long trek down to the south coast.

At school I did all the right things: I was usually top of the class, successful at exams, edited the school magazine, played the lead in the school play, and ended up being head girl, with a place at Oxford to study English. I had an inspirational English teacher, Mr Taylor, who coached me for Oxford, and I was all set for the glittering prizes.

Somehow, though, it didn't work out as planned. There was a piece of grit in the machine that I don't quite know how to characterize. It was something to do with passion – a need to be absolutely committed to some person or some thing. This was partly absorbed by literature, and partly by my passionate attachment to Hilary, who was my best friend from the third year upwards. Yet there was always a restlessness, which eventually crystallized into a religious quest in my late teens.

We were not a religious family – Christmas and Easter churchgoers – until my father's love for church music got him involved in the choir and playing the organ at the local church. Both my brothers were in the choir at different stages, but only for the pleasure of singing and to support Dad.

At home there was a lot of music. My father introduced us all to classical music, and not surprisingly I gravitated towards the romantic composers – particularly the violin concertos of Elgar, Bruch, Mendelssohn, Beethoven, Sibelius, Tchaikovsky and Brahms. It was another 20 years before I could appreciate Bach and Mozart whom he also loved. They were always 'dry sherry' or 'gin and tonic' composers to me when I wanted something altogether richer and sweeter and darker. It was the same with my passion for *Wuthering Heights*, and my incomprehension of the delights of Jane Austen.

Alongside all this was the music we shared among the four of us – my two brothers, my sister and I. I was 11 at the start of the 1960s, and my elder brother was 13. My younger sister and brother were six and seven years younger than me, but shared the same music until they moved off in their own directions. For most of my teenage years the house reverberated to the sound of the Beatles, Bob Dylan, Leonard Cohen, Simon and Garfunkel, and lots of others. We were in at the start of *Monty Python* and the other anarchic satire shows on the television, and discovered Tom Lehrer through an uncle and aunt who had some of his original recordings.

Wit and style were at a premium, and I remember many family meals around our big oak table, with friends crammed into all the interstices, the atmosphere crackling with laughter and argument. My mother's influence was strong in the area of cinema, where she inculcated in me an enthusiasm for romantic classics such as *Brief Encounter* and *Casablanca*. We shared a passion for Humphrey Bogart, Cary Grant, Gregory Peck, Leslie Howard, Ingrid Bergman, Katherine Hepburn and Bette Davis, to name but a few. Later on, my devotion shifted towards Shakespeare and the live theatre, but I never lost my love of old films.

Despite all this social and intellectual stimulation at home, and at school in the company of friends, my late teens were marred by bouts of depression and a growing sense of meaninglessness. I couldn't see what it was all for. I was obsessed by death and my fear of it, and unable to establish any reasonable basis for being alive.

I read a lot of Albert Camus and Jean-Paul Sartre and listened to Bob Dylan and Leonard Cohen, and found myself in a spiritual cul-de-sac. I took to praying to a God I didn't believe in, in the hope of some sort of sign that there was meaning to life. When an answer did come through, it came typically via music and poetry. I was 'converted' during my lower-sixth year at a Choreographic Mass to mark the opening of the new Roman Catholic cathedral in Liverpool. It came as a physical sensation of warmth, which began in the rather ice-like altar at the centre of the cathedral and then seemed to spread through my body. Somehow it conveyed to me the existence of love and meaning.

I started to go to church, but never felt very much at home. Our parish church was a very 'low' evangelical one (though I didn't know that term at the time), and it left me feeling prickly, uncomfortable and dissatisfied – aesthetically as well as spiritually. When I got to Oxford and joined OICCU (the University Christian Union), it was even worse, and I went only out of a sense of duty.

I sublimated all my religious yearnings in poetry – John Donne, George Herbert, Gerard Manley Hopkins, and T. S.

Eliot – and as a bonus discovered Dame Julian of Norwich and *The Cloud of Unknowing* when I was studying Middle English. In my second year, I suddenly felt at home and at ease with my friends and the environment, after a year of homesickness and something like culture shock. It was at this time that I met and fell in love with a third year physiologist from Whetstone, on the Northern Line.

He played bass guitar in a jazz band and knew all the Goons records off by heart. For me he played Beethoven sonatas on the piano and the blues on his acoustic guitar. He only ever had black coffee and a cigarette for breakfast, and I loved him passionately. When it went wrong, I survived to take my degree and then found a teaching job in Finland for a year to get as far away from him as I could (one of the main reasons why young female graduates take that particular job teaching English, I have since heard!).

Just before and during the Finnish period I met and corresponded with a journalist and aspiring writer I met in Southport, where my parents now lived. We had both recently had broken relationships, so we made a pact to exorcize the memories by writing novels about them and combining them in some sort of quartet, based on the four points of view of the participants. We never did combine them, but the 'exorcism' worked as we each wrote our own stories, and we grew very close in the doing of it. Marriage was discussed on one occasion when he came to visit me in Finland, but somehow it didn't fit, even though we shared many of the same beliefs and interests.

I grew very close to friends of both sexes in Finland, and fell in love with the landscape there, all of which was healing and creative. But by the time I got home I decided that I had had enough English 'conversation' to last me a lifetime, and that it was time for something more solid and weighty in terms of a career.

I couldn't decide between psychology and law, but law was financially possible because I could do it in bits while I worked to support myself. It also appealed to my sense of the dramatic (naturally I would be a famous barrister!) and my passion for justice.

I started on Part One of the Law Society exams at Liverpool Polytechnic in September 1973, working in a sleazy off-licence part time to pay the fees. I quite enjoyed my 'Jekyll and Hyde' existence, but was rapidly disillusioned with the law. Naïve as I was, I had not realized that innocence was no defence, and could not muster the stamina required to fight my way through the jungle of precedent and case law to some clarity of principle. I gave up after a term, and decided instead to go back to Oxford and see if I could get a job with Oxfam at their head office. There was a brief halcyon period at home in Southport, where all the family was together for the last time – as marriages and universities were looming – and then I was off. It was spring 1974.

Oxfam was a dynamic place to be – although my job was very menial – because the building was stuffed with intellectuals and eccentrics. I moved first to the film library and then to a liaison job in the Home Division. After two years, though, I left to write another novel.

Rosemary was the chief legacy of my Oxfam period, though other good friends remain in touch. The two of us met over the mammoth task of mounting thousands of slides for various members of staff who had been out to Oxfam projects overseas. I worked in the film library and Rosemary was in the training department, where she was responsible for arranging staff trips overseas. At this stage, we didn't discuss our faith very much, because I was becoming increasingly involved in a local charismatic church, and she attended a more traditional evangelical one in the village where she lived.

What I drew from the charismatics was the ubiquitous element in this story – passion! Initially I felt liberated by the church I attended, and set on fire by this new experience of Christianity; but the bounds grew more confining as I realized that humour and literature and music and beauty were not to be encouraged if they were not closely related to charismatic beliefs. Novels were definitely out, and anything with a critical or subversive slant, but so too were classics such as Dame Julian and *The Messiah*.

In the end it was suffocating – not least because there were 'prophecies' within the group that dictated my marriage to one of the group leaders with whom I was increasingly at odds. I grew to hate him but couldn't find a way out if I was to continue believing in charismatic principles. I was saved by my explosive temper (as has frequently happened!), which finally 'blew' over a game of Scrabble! At that point, I left him and the church group and never looked back, though I still remember with embarrassment how nauseatingly pious I was towards my family and friends during that time.

Then, in the summer of 1975, I met Sister Benedicta at the parish church prayer group, where she was doing a sort of secondment. Immediately I was drawn towards her tonic combination of warmth, subversiveness and total commitment. She seemed so much herself, so committed, yet so free.

I began to visit her at the convent more and more frequently, neglecting the novel about Finland I was supposed to be writing, and spending all my free time away from my part-time job as a nanny, doing jobs around the convent. Unobtrusively she began to introduce the future novice-mistress into our meetings, and I was 'hooked'.

Everything about the place was sweet to me. It was like a love affair with a place, with a way of life, with Sister Ben and Sister Frances, and, increasingly, with God. The silence, the holy grail-type dedication, the haunting plainchant, the incense – all of them appealed to me at such a deep, wordless level that I was powerless to resist, and longed to be there every waking minute.

My mother was horrified, as were all my family. Perhaps my father had an inkling of the attraction because he was so susceptible to the draw of beauty and music. But nothing could assuage my mother's grief and horror at what I was contemplating. She had grown up in a town that was very much split by bad feeling between Roman Catholics and Protestants; and although she had Catholic friends, she had always had a secret horror of one of her children becoming a nun. Of course, it had never seemed remotely likely. If we were anything as a family, we were Church of England, and until I met Sister Ben, none of us even knew there were Anglican nuns. Now here I was living out her worst nightmare.

I hadn't meant to tell my mother so early on, but it had just slipped out. I shall never forget that evening and that night, which we spent in storms of anger, tears and pleading. I must have seemed cruelly implacable; yet I knew I had to do it, though it was only too visible how much pain I was causing her. She saw it as a denial of all she stood for, a rejection of family life. Now I have children of my own her reaction makes sense to me. Not then.

I joined the convent at the end of January 1976. I can't remember how I got there, though I think I insisted on going alone. It was less than six months after my first encounter with Sister Ben. I was twenty-six.

It wasn't long before I discovered that my romantic vision of the life did not constitute reality. I was buoyed up in the novitiate by my devotion to the novice-mistress, but after first vows in 1978, I was out of her protection and the real battles began, as described earlier.

The whole experience, though, was a proving ground; it made me work out what was important to me. In the dark hours of silence in the chapel before the day began, I gradually faced my fears of death and loneliness. I learned that I wasn't the easy-going, charming person I had thought I was, but someone with strong views and deep physical and emotional needs – and a lot of anger.

When I finally burst out (leaving the community with some wounds too, I'm afraid), my relationship with God was at least honest. I hadn't yet encountered the feminist critique of Christianity, which has since nourished me, but I had irrevocably lost any Anglican sense of being on my best behaviour with God, along with my romanticism about religion.

I also spent an enormous amount of effort struggling to reconcile the traditional monastic doctrines with touchstones drawn from literature and music. So often the monastic values, or at least my community's version of monastic values, seemed to lose out by contrast. They felt artificial, imposed from outside, while the songs and the poems seemed to be reverberating inside, like a tuning fork. I remember once brushing the sanctuary carpet during my time as chapel novice, singing some fragments of a Bob Dylan song 'Just Like a Woman' to myself, reduced to tears by the accuracy of its description of my inner life.

I was obsessed by connecting it all up: everything that rang true for me, everything that expressed any human truth, had to fit into the scheme. I attacked any theological systems or monastic mores that did not allow for this inclusive approach, and read voraciously to try and make sense of the rationale behind religious life.

I read Lorenz on animal behaviour and Goffman on 'total institutions' to try and understand the conditioning which went on in the novitiate, and the socio-psychological reasons for some of the more bizarre community customs. I remember being particularly enlightened and amused by Lorenz's definition of bowing as appeasement behaviour.

Almost all our theological study in the community was in the area of spirituality and devotion, but I managed to lay my hands on some more radical theology from one of the professed sisters who had an intellectual bent (and access to a library). There were only thrillers and romances in the fiction section of the convent library, so there was no chance of any literary stimulation, but I knew a lot of poetry by heart, and this sustained me. I also found myself writing a lot of poetry – to counteract the intellectual and emotional bleakness of the life.

In the end, of course, as explained earlier, I was delivered over to Wendy Robinson and the Jungian framework of ideas found in psychotherapy which gave me the crucial tools to understand what was going on.

It was only a few months later that I met Dom Wilfrid.

David, as he was christened, had come to the monastic life by a very different route, and had also been there 16 years longer than me when we met. In many ways, his early life was much more extraordinary than mine.

His father, William Valentine Weston, was born in 1867 (almost 20 years before my maternal granny) and spent 25 years of his life in imperial India, with the Bengal Silk Company. In his leisure hours he was an animal collector, polo player and game-hunter, or passed his time at the local gentlemen's club which was a Volunteer company of the Calcutta Light Horse. The club was peopled by Scottish expatriates like himself, and he seems to have led a very congenial life, with many servants at his beck and call.

When the First World War broke out, he returned to England and joined up, hoping to command Indian cavalry, but in the event spent the war training younger men for the Western

Front. After the war, his thoughts turned to ordination. A younger brother, Frank, was well known as the Anglo-Catholic Bishop of Zanzibar, and he himself entertained thoughts of returning to India as a missionary.

He trained at Chichester theological College in the 1920s (Frank died while he was there) and did one of his two curacies at Burgess Hill, Sussex, where he met and fell in love with a certain Gertrude Erby, who was the organist there. After a brief courtship, they were married in 1934. He was 66 and she 29!

Major the Reverend W.V. Weston was appointed Rector of the small rural parish of Edburton beneath the South Downs, and there their first son, Frank, was born in 1935, to the great delight of his aged father. After two years, David was born. Sixteen days later, his father died on Christmas Eve, the day before his 70th birthday – not a very propitious start for the family.

Following his father's death, David and his mother and Frank had to move out of the beautiful spacious rectory at Edburton; they then settled in Brighton. They lived with David's maternal grandfather, who had been a dentist by profession, and had not approved of his son-in-law – only a few years his junior.

By all accounts, Mr W. H. Erby was a stern Victorian figure and David was periodically beaten, though surprisingly he maintains there was never any injustice in the beatings and even seems to feel that his grandfather had a grudging pleasure in his exploits, which proved he wasn't a typical 'parson's boy'.

David's mother preferred the company of elderly ladies and aged couples, and both boys remember interminable 'genteel teas' in darkened rooms, only alleviated by a half-crown pressed into their palms as they left. They weren't allowed to 'play out', and both of them went away to school (different ones) at the age of nine, so they had no friends in Brighton to return to in the holidays.

By his own admission, David was a restless, active boy, frequently getting into scrapes, falling out of trees and into ponds in his pursuit of birds and butterflies and rare flowers, which were his passion. Unlike his brother Frank, he was not bookish, and was prone to fidget in church where their mother was the organist. They went morning and evening every Sunday from a very young age, and added early morning communion after they were confirmed. Their grandfather only went on special occasions such as Remembrance Day.

David has very early memories of Frank leading family prayers, but although they were surrounded by religion and lived in the shadow of the Bishop of Zanzibar as well as their father, David does not seem to have reflected very deeply about God or the meaning of life. There was no adolescent crisis, because faith and churchgoing were taken for granted.

David was shy and reserved at school although he enjoyed team games, representing his school, and became Captain of his House. Although he resisted the school's pressure to be ordained, he did feel sufficiently drawn to the Franciscans to become a Companion of St Francis. He was impressed by their austerity and commitment but still could not see himself conducting missions and preaching, so he left school with the future unresolved.

He then did his national service in Cyprus and came back to London to an inheritance of £5,000 from an aunt. Still unsure what to do, he got a job as a managerial trainee for a catalogue firm in the city, and compensated for the boredom of it with a new Ford Consul convertible and an Italian girlfriend!

It seems to have been a very innocent year abroad in London, which he frequently refers to as his 'annus mirabilis'. But again, he was drifting, and during that year – 1959 – he suddenly came under the influence of an older man who had just left Mirfield. It was almost as if he saw David as a substitute vocation, to assuage his own guilt. David was then attending All Saints, Margaret Street (he had been 'entrusted' to the curate there by his own priest in Brighton), where the atmosphere was conducive to 'vocation'. After listening to a sermon at Margaret Street preached by the then abbot of Nashdom, he was overwhelmed by a sense of vocation to the monastic life, which focused all his latent idealism.

He was introduced to the Benedictines at Nashdom Abbey by his brother Frank, who was by that time an oblate there. Immediately he knew that if he had to enter a community, then this was the one, because he knew he could fulfil what was required. He wouldn't have to go out or preach to anyone, or 'perform' in any way. He felt that all that was needed was endurance and determination, and he knew he had both in abundance. Here at last was something to which he could give himself totally and which would use what he perceived to be his gifts.

The community welcomed him with open arms because he was the great Frank Weston's nephew and the brother of one of their oblates. Even now he feels they might have questioned him a bit more critically so that his motives would have been revealed – if only to himself. Instead, it was all quickly settled, and he had a few months to sort out his affairs before the agreed entry date in January 1960.

Christmas was full of a sense of doom. His mother was against it, though not violently (coming round to the idea quite soon). His girlfriend seemed to accept it, and soon David was drawn in, full of a sense of inevitability.

He took the name of Wilfrid (his second baptismal name) as there was already a David in community, and set out to be 'a perfect monk'. Not for him the outbursts and rebellions that characterized my five years in the convent! From 1960 to 1965 he submerged himself in the Rule of St Benedict and set himself to be meticulous in his observances. Pictures of him from that time show clearly the ascetic expression and self-effacing demeanour that all monks and nuns are supposed to acquire. He even had the perfect bone structure for the part. His head, when shaved, looked more austere and beautiful than it did with hair.

One of the more complex characters in the community took over the ordination training programme when Wilfrid reached that stage, after taking solemn vows in 1964, and exerted a sort of 'Svengali' influence over him, grooming him for high office, with himself always there at his shoulder. The good part of the arrangement was that he made Wilfrid think and question for the first time in his life. He was 30 in his own estimation, before any real intellectual awakening began. Soon after his ordination as deacon in 1967, he was sent out to preach and teach, and found to his surprise that he could do both. By then, he had been hidden away for eight years and had been continuously fed with theology, rule and discipline; it seemed he was able to present it with little difficulty, and even some success.

Yet although intellectually awake, he was still a sleepwalker in terms of any real emotional investment in his role. To use his later terminology, 'David' was still asleep, though 'Wilfrid' was performing efficiently. Once he was ordained, his rise through the community was meteoric. He was made assistant novice-master in 1969, novice-master three months later, prior in 1971, and abbot in 1974 – the youngest superior in the Anglican religious orders.

I have a vague memory of attending a novitiate seminar at my own community two or three years after he was made abbot when I was a very junior novice. There were about ten of us (collected from neighbouring communities) crammed into a sort of summer-house, and he 'lectured' to us about basic communities for about twenty minutes. I remember being unimpressed by the talk, as it seemed too stiff and old-fashioned, when the subject was dynamic, experimental communities and his audience was small and intimate. I was impressed, though, by his ascetic bearing and his long, sensitive fingers!

His time as novice-master exposed him, briefly, to the culture of the 1960s, as novices were coming in with the music and the books and the revolutionary attitudes of that time. As the monks had not been allowed to watch television or listen to the radio, he had not been aware of the ferment outside. He now began to identify himself with this new outlook, this questioning of the old authorities and the search for 'real' community. He began tentatively to see himself as a radical. However, this was problematical for him, as the traditional teaching of obedience, hiddenness and self-abnegation had provided him with the framework he needed to develop his strengths.

The potential split in his psyche did not really emerge until he was made abbot. As prior, his talent for practical work was allowed its head, and he was deeply involved in the building of a new extension to the house, spending much time in absorbed consultation with builders, architects and craftsmen. It was an aspect of the life that he really enjoyed.

The traditional monastic emphasis on manual work had previously given him lots of opportunities to indulge his other passion – gardening – and had sanctioned his desire to be out of the limelight. But as abbot, he was dragged from obscurity and thrust into the role of bridging the ever-increasing gap between the old guard and the stormtroopers of renewal. Vatican II (1962–5) was making its presence felt ever more strongly now in the Anglican communities, and was exacerbating the old divisions. Wilfrid saw his task as primarily one of reconciliation, and he set about it with characteristic dedication.

It may be that his temperament was not extrovert enough to achieve this end, or that his own austerity and perfectionism aroused resentment and guilt rather than emulation. Obviously, I cannot speak for his fellow monks, but his diary for that time records something of the battles that raged around him. Suffice it to say that by the time he and I met at Vauxhall – six years into his abbacy – he had already consigned his personal feelings to the 'deep-freeze' and was resigned to passing on the tradition intact to the next generation.

With his election as abbot – and even before as prior and novice-master – he was given much more freedom of movement, and became exposed to the company of women in a way he was totally unprepared for. He was 'Confessor Extraordinary' and 'Major Superior' to several female communities, which meant seeing all the sisters individually on a regular basis (as well as more formal duties); and he was also spiritual director to lay women and oblates.

He admits to being very naïve about the effect he had on them and vice versa. Nothing had prepared him for dealing with strong emotion from women, for his relationship with his Italian girlfriend in 1959 had been very chaste and innocent. At times he found all this quite hard to handle, and his natural sympathy for women lacked the maturity that comes from experience. No doubt the memory of such encounters contributed to his desire to put his emotions on ice; but by far the most important emotional event in his life prior to our meeting was the death of his mother in the autumn of 1979.

His reactions to her death were complicated, and it took some time for him to understand what was happening to him. Although there was little overt affection between them, she had his unswerving loyalty, and everything he did was unconsciously referred to her. While she was alive there was always a home to go to, and with her death he felt as if his sheet-anchor had gone. What was he doing? What was his life about? Who was he living for?

It was like an adolescent crisis and a mid-life crisis rolled into one. Wilfrid had never wanted to upset her, and so had never questioned what he was doing with his life, even when he was unhappy. But now, suddenly, he had only himself as a reference point.

When we met a year later, none of this was visible, probably even to himself, until I had the temerity to question the morality, and even the humanity, of his 'deep-freeze solution'.

And our story began.

4

Oxford and Suffolk

After leaving the community, my first days and weeks with Rosemary were about learning a new structure for my days, one that wasn't imposed from above. Virginia Woolf – in another context – called it 'the business of getting from breakfast to dinner'. It was a frightening business, in my case.

Rosemary, though, had planned things carefully to ease me back into some kind of normal life. I remember her deeply casual hints about some new eye make-up that they had just got in at Marks & Spencer's. And there were visits to some wonderfully bland, non-threatening films, which neither of us would be seen dead at these days. She even nursed me through one or two social events, where the questions about what I did were potential minefields.

In the early days of March 1981, a letter arrived from Wilfrid, suggesting a meeting, and enclosing a poem he had written the previous week, influenced by the card I had sent him with hands cradling a baby:

> Cradled in tenderness
> cherished with faithfulness
> cupped in the hands of your love
> waking to joyfulness
> raised now from lifelessness
> reborn with a birth from above.
>
> Yours is this gift to me
> this strange new power to see
> led now from blindness to sight
> taught by this mystery
> how to love tenderly
> emerging from darkness to light.
>
> Moulded from earth and clay
> called now from night to day
> dying to come to new birth
> help me walk this way
> lit by this glorious ray
> shedding its radiance on earth.

He apologized for the 'prosaic' quality of his letter, saying that he had much to say, but wanted to wait until we were face to face. He suggested that for our first meeting it would be better if we were on our own, and offered to drive to Suffolk to see me. He said that 15th or 16th March would be the best day for him. He concluded with the lines, 'It is very good to know that you have come through recent events unscathed, and that you have the hope and the energy for the next stage.'

By this time, I had already been to see Philippa's parents' cottage in Suffolk, and it was everything I could have wished for: beautiful, old, quiet, in a small village – so not completely isolated – and near the sea. Unfortunately there were practical matters to sort out, so I had to possess my soul in patience.

When things finally began to move, everything happened at once: I acquired a car and a dog within a few days of each other. The car was planned, of course, not to say overdue, but the dog was an addition to my list of treasured things. She was six years old, house-trained, fond of travel, and a most human-looking Cavalier King Charles Spaniel. Her name was Fleur; I wrote and told Wilfrid about her.

When I finally arrived in 'The Cottage on the Common' in Westleton, near Dunwich, a welcoming letter from Wilfrid was waiting on the mat. There was the usual enclosure, but this time it was almost like a litany or a hymn to joy:

My love and thoughts and prayers go with you always
May you find joy and delight in all things
in the companionship, devotion and fidelity of Fleur
and in the rhythm of your days.

May you rejoice in your cottage, and in all that is about you.
in plants and trees and flowers
in the gardens and hedgerows, in the fields and woods
May you rejoice in the sea in all its moods, and upon the sea-shore
in the birds in their song
in the animals wild and tame, and in the small creatures
May a Benedicite resound in your own heart
as the whole creation unites to sing its canticle of joy to the Lord.

His letter began with the words 'Greetings to you after the Exodus'. What more could I have wished for in a welcoming letter? And yet my feelings were still sealed off somewhere where they could not be reached or awakened. I felt pleasure, but it did not touch the panic-stricken sense of homesickness that afflicted me for the first night and day. There was straightforward fear too – not helped by the sight of an axe, obviously carefully placed on the floor beside the bed in case of intruders!

My greatest need was to be mothered, held, cradled. I was in no mood to sing a hymn of joy to a God who seemed to have absented himself. Also, there was no longer any reason to pretend: my only hope of survival was to be honest about my reactions – wherever they took me.

My days at the cottage were drawn into some kind of pattern by the necessity of feeding and walking Fleur – a tremendous boon, as I had been so afraid of lack of structure, and empty days with too much time to think – even though I had in theory gone to the cottage to do just that. My afternoons were filled with regular work on a new novel (which I never looked at again after I left the cottage), and in the mornings I pottered about doing domestic jobs, shopping and writing letters.

The most healing thing was the space, and the freedom to walk for miles without meeting a soul. The wide emptiness of the sky and the seashore restored to me some of the uncomplicated faith of my youth. Even the church where I went each Sunday seemed open to the sky, as the windows were plain glass, transparent to the greenness all around. It was nearly Easter, and the air was full of softness and warmth.

The car, too, was a great source of joy. It was a black Morris 1300 (like the 1100 in shape) with red upholstery, low mileage on the clock, and a price tag of only £350. Fleur loved it from the word go, and used to sit eagerly on the front passenger seat ready to set off, even when I was just washing it! We explored the country lanes in it for miles around, luxuriating in our freedom.

It was about half-way through my time at the cottage that I was also able to finalize plans for a holiday in Greece. This was the realization of a dream held since schooldays, when ancient Greece had been my passion. Luckily, Rosemary shared my enthusiasm, and my father (in a rash moment!) had promised to pay for the trip as he was so pleased that I was out of the convent.

The only date that was suitable was at the beginning of May, so it meant that I would in the event, spend less than a month in Suffolk. Wilfrid had hoped to come to the cottage in the first week of May, so our plans had to be revised yet again. By this time, I was beginning to wonder if our meeting would ever materialize.

Obviously Wilfrid could not suddenly announce to the monks that he was having a day off to go and see 'a woman', so all our plans had to be woven around the fixed events in his diary. There were conferences, sermons, visits to other communities, and because he was the abbot, nobody questioned what he did with his spare hours between engagements. A small resentful part of me remembered how different it was for a novice or a junior sister, having to account for her use of time, the money she spent, and any gifts she received. But I said none of this to Wilfrid, knowing it was inappropriate to our developing relationship, which was based so much on trust and mutual encouragement.

It gradually became clear that it would not be possible for us to meet in Suffolk, which was a great disappointment as he had formed such a clear picture of the cottage and I wanted to meet him in a place that had become my own. Instead it was decided that 27 April, the day after my return from Suffolk, was the best day, and that we would meet near the church in my parents' Berkshire village of Kintbury (they had moved there in the late '70s because of my father's promotion). If it was wet, we could meet in Rosemary's flat in Oxford.

As the time approached, our letters were full of apprehension on each side – we were each afraid of disappointing the other. I was afraid that his idealistic picture of me would be disappointed by the reality – both physical and emotional. He was afraid that my knowledge of him – based almost entirely on intuition and letters – would be shown to be without foundation. Yet despite these qualms, his last letter before our meeting was full of joy and humour – and a £5 note was enclosed to pay for any particular delicacies that Fleur and I might find indispensable for our picnic lunch together –

'smoked swordfish, or clam chowder or pickled walnuts, or a choice bone'!

Meanwhile, I was trying hard to hold on to the time I had left at the cottage, and all these plans were wishing it away. The weather was good, and Fleur and I were out a lot enjoying the sunshine – and, in her case, the rabbits. I seemed to spend a disproportionate amount of time hauling her by her tail out of the rabbit holes in the sand dunes! But it was good to see her so independent and wilful. Her wilfulness was strangely important to me then, because I was finding it hard to cope with any kind of devotion – even in a dog.

I wrote in my journal at the time how I wished sometimes that she was a more haughty, reserved sort of dog – anything, in fact, but a spaniel! This seems almost comical in retrospect, but any kind of intensity during that time made me feel trapped and crowded. Even when a special friend came to stay, one I had been most close to in the London period, there were moments when I felt frightened by the empathy and the affection between us. And when my family came to stay with me over Easter, I reacted with irritation and impatience much of the time – though I was immediately overwhelmed by loneliness when they left.

I think all this must have been another aspect of my reaction to the intensity of feeling that had precipitated my departure from the community. It seems as if something in me was backing off from emotion at a great rate, but at the same time there was also the child-like need.

I wrote the following words in my journal:

20 April 1981 – Journal Entry

> I need love so much . . . But I need the man or woman to be MUTE, or almost! Grave, independent, reserved and yet sensitive and responsive at appropriate times. Wise, humorous, full of his own concerns (no need to be entertained) and deeply caring about the world and its problems, knowledgeable and rooted in eternity, so nothing really flaps him, yet also passionate!!

This was almost a portrait of Wilfrid as he turned out to be, yet at the time I was full of apprehension – and not just about him.

He had not seen me without my habit and veil. My hair had gone much darker in the community, and he might not like the jeans or dungarees I habitually wore. Yet I didn't want to move into fashionable clothes yet, as I didn't feel I knew how to walk in a feminine way anymore and I hadn't yet found a style that suited my new sense of myself, tentative as that was. I had a bright red shirt and some denim dungarees, and they were the only statement I was capable of making, but they didn't seem right for a romantic encounter somehow.

Friday 23 April 1981 – Journal Entry

Three more days in the cottage, four more days until we meet. Have been reading *Ring of Bright Water* by Gavin Maxwell, which I found in the cottage. Describes my condition so well – both the sense of lostness and the aggression: 'Every living creature exists by a routine of some kind: the small rituals of that routine are land marks, the boundaries of security, the *reassuring walls* that exclude a *horror vacui* [my italics]; thus in our own species, after some tempest of the spirit in which the landmarks seem to have been swept away, a man will reach out tentatively in mental darkness to feel the walls, to assure himself that they still stand where they stood – a necessary gesture, for the walls are of his own building, without universal reality; and what man makes he may destroy . . . As among human beings animal insecurity may manifest itself as aggression or humility, ill-temper or ill-health or an excessive affection for a parental figure.'

Reminded me of the brick-dust, and what Wendy said, in another context, of the need to build a ship for the spirit, something of my own making, a vessel to contain all the things which are dear to me.

I left the 'Cottage-on-the-Common' the following Monday with a sense of loss, but the awareness that I had at least laid the foundations of my own structure for living.

5
The Downs and the River

The following is part of a letter I received from Wilfrid after our planned meeting:

Tuesday, 28 April 1981

> As I left you yesterday my heart was filled with gratitude and joy . . . Sitting talking in the little house [Rosemary's Oxford flat – it was wet], walking beside the stream and across the fields, talking in the car, all these taken together had a wholeness to which house, fields and car were incidental, though appropriate. How can I thank you for being the essence of that wholeness? When the time came to part it seemed right and good and true. Partly it was the manner of our parting, partly it was, as we said earlier, because there was the sense that it was in the hands of God, partly it had been such a perfect day . . .
>
> How can I thank you? Only, I think, by that combination of love and freedom which you encourage me to believe is an acceptable offering.

His letter was also full of his delight at discovering that I was not 22, as he had thought, but nearly 32 – thus not half his age, but a respectable 12 years younger! The 'pristine' look he had perceived in me (presumably at Vauxhall) was no doubt due to the convent phenomenon of magically preserving the skin wrinkle-free!

My memories of the day are much more fragmented and down to earth. I remember the paté, cheese and wine on Rosemary's dining table; the breaking of one of her favourite wine glasses; my own inability to eat much because of a stomach upset – which I couldn't bring myself to mention as it seemed so prosaic. I remember intense joy too, of course, but more like bursts of sunlight among racing clouds.

There was a poem included with Wilfrid's letter – the first for a few weeks. It contained a verse from his early poem about Vauxhall, where he spoke of 'adjacent hands', and went on to develop the theme to quite a different, almost ecstatic, conclusion (verses 5 and 6):

> Then the heart leaps, though not at sight or sound
> but at a knowing that warms and soothes and heals
> coaxing to life the small, clear flame of joy
> proclaiming the heart a tabernacle where God's Glory dwells.

> The moment passes, but if the memory should fade
> the body bears the marks of that encounter;
> marks that no eye can see
> marks that do not need the senses' confirmation.

Two days later, he was writing in a very different tone:

30 April 1981

> Today the life-defeating, love-denying spectres
> have rattled their bones at me.
> Knowing that their sovereignty over my death
> has been challenged by life,
> with chilly fingers they beckon me back
> into their cold oblivion.

The other three verses were full of affirmation that love would triumph, using the image of Michelangelo's famous painting of God and Adam with outstretched fingers touching, but emphasizing Eve's part in the continuing creation of Adam and the world, in her role as Sophia. In the note accompanying the letter, there was no explanation of the circumstances that gave rise to the poem, beyond a comment that 'yesterday proved a difficult, painful day'.

Wilfrid then went to Rome, at the Pope's invitation, to be present at the beatification of a Trappist nun, and his letter from there contained a detailed account of the ceremony, and his meeting with the Pope, but nothing personal, except a card of the 'fingertips' from the Sistine Chapel. In any case, by this time I had set off for Greece, so I didn't get his letter until I returned, where it waited with another one.

Greece with Rosemary was all I had hoped for, with the temples of Athene and Apollo at Delphi a particular revelation. I was stirred by the way the ancient Greeks chose such dramatic natural sites for their temples, as if instinctively fusing the best in both nature and religion. It seemed very different from the instinctive suppression of nature in certain aspects of Christianity. Perhaps it was also the way the temples were open to the sky, and the intense white light.

Less good was the way we seemed to attract kerb-crawlers in Athens. We were pursued by a 'flasher' down the site of the Agora, and even on the quiet island of Tinos, where we spent our second week, we were constantly being leered at and invited to nudist beaches. Twice Rosemary was forced to point out to me that I was no longer wearing a habit and therefore couldn't any longer smile at people indiscriminately!

The second letter from Wilfrid, which awaited my return, introduced an idea that became a pivotal one for him in those later summer months when he was struggling to sort out what his love for me meant for his vocation. Evidently during our day together I had put my finger on 'the crucial point' – which was the possibility of 'David and Wilfrid meeting and coalescing'.

Perhaps it was the dawning of my own dim awareness that I had fallen in love with a monk, and discovered it was a man who was responding. This only became a real issue for me two years later, but for Wilfrid it was just about to come to the boil. The two names had come to stand for different aspects of himself, exemplified by his pre- and post-community selves. Yet at this stage, his thinking on the subject was only just developing. Interestingly, he had signed his card from Rome with an inverted heart, which he said was a 'W' becoming a 'D'. Another strand in his reflection on our relationship also began to emerge in his letter:

> I am more determined than ever that my love for you should never restrict you or limit you in any way. Like a numbered Swiss Bank Account, it is there to be drawn upon when you feel the need. You may prefer to forget about it except in emergency, or you may draw upon it regularly. I cannot claim that it is a matter of indifference to me which you decide upon; it is not. But basically I love you because you are you, and not because I want to benefit from this loving.

My own thinking about the future was oscillating wildly at this stage, and it was this that he was picking up on in my letters and trying to respond to. It must have been hard, as one minute I was talking of joining a kibbutz (just at the moment when Israel was on the verge of war with Syria – as he rather dryly pointed out), while the next I was talking of training to be a deaconess. Other schemes that were in favour at the time were going to Africa or working in religious broadcasting.

What I actually did was to go to Ullapool in the Western Highlands, for a week's holiday with my family. It was not quite so exotic as my other schemes, but it was a place that had played a large part in my fantasies of wildness and freedom during the convent years. I had worked there in the year between school and university, and this was my first return visit.

Wilfrid, meanwhile, was pondering on whether the community were likely to be noticing any change in him:

4 June 1981

> . . . to what extent people see any change in me, I do not know, but life seems very different. You do, in effect, exercise a gentle ascesis which prevents it all from being a self-indulgence on my part. Perhaps when I would like a letter from you you do not write; or perhaps when you write you do not say all that I would like you to say. But, at the same time, I know that this is good. I love you and I trust you; I love God and I trust him. The two loves and the two trusts are inseparable . . .

In his next letter (14 June) – the first of quite a series to be written in the early hours of the morning, after a sleepless night – he commented with some wit on the whole question of camouflage, and how it was possible to hide the startling change that had taken place in him. His comments were prompted by the sight of a white cat in the dawn light:

14 June 1981

> It is nearly 4.00 a.m., and outside it is almost light, light enough to see, a moment or so ago, a white cat stalking through the garden a hundred yards away. How frustrating it must be to be a white cat; he must need special skills to compensate for his lack of camouflage. But, who knows, perhaps there is much kudos in the cat world from being white.

Further on, he made the point that he was usually 'reticent, private and secretive to a fault' (so perhaps camouflage would not come too hard to him), but he was obviously somewhat torn between welcoming the lack of inhibition he felt towards me and deploring the 'dangerously permanent' form of letters in which it was expressed. Perhaps the more cautious 'Wilfrid' was beginning to put a check on the exuberance of 'David'. Certainly it was a necessary caution – even if occasionally I chafed against it – because every time he was absent from Nashdom Abbey, his letters were routinely opened by the prior.

By now, we were both feeling the need of face-to-face communication, and Thursday, 2 July, seemed viable as he would be able to break his journey to York (to attend the Advisory Council for Anglican Religious Communities) at Kintbury and spend the day with me, as before. In the meantime, he continued to chronicle his thoughts in poems. One written on 10 June was replying to an old theme of mine:

> once you dismissed, smilingly
> Some words of mine concerning you
> saying that I was biased in your favour . . .

He answered that, yes, he was biased, if that adjective was used to describe the perception that stems from seeing as God sees:

> But if I aspire to see as God sees
> then in love truth is revealed.
> Tender, compassionate and warm,
> God does not gaze; rather he
> upholds all things in being
> by the power of his creating and redeeming love.

Perversely, at that time, I wanted only a man's love: earthy, passionate and flawed. The convent experience I had just fought off so painfully was all about loving as God loves, and I had found it both unworkable and untenable. These days I would simply put it the other way round: that anything which is fully human is of God.

But for Wilfrid, of course – struggling to integrate his monastic vocation with this new human love – it was imperative that the two should be seen to come from the same source, and the one be subsumed in the other.

We met for the second time since Vauxhall on Thursday, 2 July. As before, I picked him up in the early morning at Kintbury station, but this time the weather was good, so instead of heading for Oxford and Rosemary's flat we set off for the Berkshire Downs. Much of the day was spent walking hand in hand through the waist-high grass along the Ridgeway, revelling in the breadth of hills and the complete anonymity. At lunchtime, we savoured the opposite pleasure of being alone in a crowd, eating our bread and cheese in a remote country pub among the locals.

The high point of the day was when we sat down to rest somewhere in a soft undulation of hills, and ended up – for the first time – in each other's arms. Had we been less complicated and less scrupulous creatures, we might have made love there and then, but there were too many religious inhibitions on both sides. Despite the absence of any visible reminders of Wilfrid's vows (he had come in casual clothes), there was no way of forgetting their reality.

Wilfrid's letter, the next day, was ecstatic, thanking me for a day that was 'perfect in every way'. I too was conscious of joy, but even more of relief that some physical communication had been established. It allayed my fears that I was being idealized and internalized, transmuted into something 'rich and strange' that could live in a monastery. I was also very torn. I had seen enough of the effect that a secret relationship could have on others in a community. It could spread a sort of pollution – 'lilies that fester smell far worse than weeds'.

Yet the relationship had its own momentum, and I dared to believe that we would both strive to protect its integrity. If it ever got beyond Wilfrid's power to keep to his vows, he would either have to finish the relationship or leave his community. I didn't like where that left me, but that was my choice, as I well knew.

I was both glad and amused to receive, on 4 July, a second letter about our day together, which expressed the difficulty he had had 'in containing his own physical reactions':

4 July 1981

According to the laws of thermo-dynamics I ought to have exploded, melted or disappeared in a cloud of steam. But such laws seemed to have been in abeyance for the day, and I survive to reflect upon it.

His letter did go on, as usual, to reflect upon it, and produced an interesting response to my unease about the prevailing religious language and symbolism in his poems. He said he needed to be sure that he was offering me a 'real genuine love' that could come from the whole of himself and 'not just a submerged part . . . that could not bear close scrutiny'. (A love where David and Wilfrid were integrated?) A postscript to the letter showed that he too had been struggling with the implications of our day together. For both of us, this first real physical expression of our feelings had forced some sort of assessment of where we were heading. In Wilfrid's case, the split had begun to appear again:

> I have been trying to face up to the truth with as much honesty as possible. There is no doubt I love you very much. In my eyes you are perfect in every way . . . Now my difficulty is that although as David I can say that, in what sense can I do so as Wilfrid, and all that name represents? Although I love you as totally as Wilfrid as I do as David, there are complications which I do not need to spell out.
>
> Is it enough for you, satisfactory for you, fair to you, that I should just love you in this way, that can in practical terms offer you so little? Is love worth having that cannot progress beyond a certain point? Might it not just be a blind alley, distracting you from relationships that could be for you fulfilling in every way?
>
> This does not imply a limitation of my love for you, but rather factors beyond my control. My love for you is the only absolute that I have known in my life, the only overwhelmingly true thing that has happened to me. Beside it, all else is experimental, partial, conditional.

This thought that he might be holding me back from more satisfactory relationships was obviously very much on his mind, because it resurfaced in a poem a fortnight later, after a gap in our communication while I spent time with two old friends from Finland. He seemed to be preparing himself to 'stand aside', and the imagery of the poem (17 July) was to reverberate through our relationship for a long time to come:

17 July 1981

> In the fairy-tale it is the Prince who
> kisses the Princess into wakefulness,
> but in reality it is my great and humble task,
> as a servant of that house,
> to fulfil this part before the Prince comes.
>
> Then I shall be content to watch,
> like a stage-hand in the wings,
> the intricacies of the 'pas-de-deux',
> able to delight in the supreme expression of that art.
> Content to be a 'props man' beside the stage,
> where Prince and Princess step out the figures of the dance.
>
> And when the performance ends, and they pass from sight,
> there will be no envy in my heart,
> for I shall recall that I too had my part
> As the mayfly had his day of glory . . .

I don't think I appreciated at the time how much it cost him to contemplate renouncing 'the only overwhelmingly true thing' that had happened to him. It smacked too much of the Abraham/Isaac story, which had been my personal bugbear in the religious life, and prevented me from going all out for my own 'selfish' happiness. What I wanted from Wilfrid was not that he should heroically give me up, but that he should fight to keep me – even if I wasn't totally sure that I wanted to keep him.

My emotions continued to oscillate, with my strongest desires being for a place of my own and a satisfying job. I was still living at my parents' home, and finding it hard to spend my life waiting: waiting for Social Security to produce some money; waiting for a job to come up; waiting for letters from Wilfrid. I needed to be up and doing, but didn't know where to start.

Our next meeting was to follow fast upon the last. We had decided on what Wilfrid called 'a Rat and Mole "Wind in the

Willows" sort of day'. He was quite clear that it should be on the water or in the water, depending on the temperature. If *on* the water, a river would be best, as it would be easier to hire a boat. His letter of 24 July is an example of the clandestine, rather tongue-in-cheek sort of arrangements we were obliged to make at this stage:

24 July 1981

> David Valentine (his third Christian name) will arrive in Newbury by train at 5.56 p.m. on Thursday, 30 July, and will stay that night at the Queen's Hotel, Market Place, Newbury, where his phone number will be Newbury 47447. He will arrive in Kintbury next morning at 9.23 a.m. at the latest.
>
> He seems quite calm about it all, but a cardiograph would belie his apparent composure.

This was the time of the Royal Wedding, 1981, with street parties both in my parents' village and in Torquay where Wilfrid was staying with his sister-in-law's family – so romance was definitely in the air. At long last Friday, 1 August, dawned, and he was there at 9.23 a.m., as promised.

We drove to Wallingford and hired a small cabin-cruiser for the afternoon. Part of me felt it was a very extravagant gesture to spend £25 (more than I received in a week from Social Security) on ensuring privacy and tranquillity for ourselves, but another part of me loved it. It was a warm day, and we were safe from prying eyes.

I remember that it was that day that we discovered our mutual love for Laurence Whistler's poems, and his book about his brief idyllic marriage to Jill Furse (*The Initials in the Heart*). From then on, these poems – and even episodes from their life together (cut short by her death) – took on an almost iconic status in our own story. We began to speak of our brief, snatched meetings as 'lives', in the same way as they spoke of his all-too-brief periods of leave during the Second World War. We both knew sections of the poems by heart, and I remember exactly where we were – outside a pub in Wallingford – when we discovered this strange congruity in our tastes.

Wilfrid had read *The Initials in the Heart* in a book club edition in the abbey library, which was without photographs, so I was able to fill in lots of physical details about the two of them that he had not known. Discovering that we had both treasured the same relatively obscure book gave us a deeper sense that our own meeting was meant to be, and that our feelings for each other were part of some greater plan.

The day lives in my memory as peaceful and unruffled, just like the river itself, but perhaps that is as much the effect of Wilfrid's poem about it as the accuracy of my memory:

> Calm, peaceful river:
> between green banks its quiet waters flow,
> Down this broad stream,
> beside the water-meadows
> and the bank-side trees
> past the discreet houses with their smooth lawns
> our small boat floats by.
>
> Companioned by duck and swan,
> by moorhen, coot and grebe
> we accept the slower pace of this other world
> sweetly attuned to its tranquillity.

In deference, I am sure, to my insistence on 'reality', Wilfrid also describes the other, unseen, faces of our river:

> Mud flats, docks and cranes,
> factories and power stations,
> industrial effluent and town sewers
> are part of this river's truth,
>
> but these do not invalidate
> this brief interlude of a summer's afternoon
> when with my heart's love
> I share the beauty of this river scene.

The penultimate verse shows very clearly that he doesn't expect the idyll to last much longer, as it moves into a distinctly elegiac mood:

For all my other days, weeks, months, and years
shall give me time enough
to explore, alone, the other qualities and moods
of life's varied stream.

His first letter after our day on the river was written on 6 August, a few days before the poem, but it explored the same mood:

6 August 1981

I do want to affirm what a joy it has been to love you, and how creative it has been for me. Of that I can speak affirmatively. What I do not understand is what happens now. Does one bring it to a nice tidy end, with a lowering of flags to bugle calls on the anniversary of our first day at St Peters [Vauxhall]? Do we become all detached and matter of fact, and meet occasionally for coffee?

. . . I have lost my boundary marks or my bearings, or both! I know that I can solve the problem by a simple decision, but somehow it seems more important now that one's life is guided not so much by arbitrary decisions, but rather by the perception of truth.

He suggested another meeting, ten days on, to 'clarify a few points'. Yet it was obvious from the general tone of the letter that he was contemplating making an end. The next day he restarted his letter (though he included his first attempt), and it quickly became clear that he was finding it increasingly difficult to hold the David and Wilfrid personas together:

7 August 1981

I tend to feel that the instinct to analyse, justify and explain which seems so strong in me now is less a matter of temperament and more one of circumstances. Certainly the David Weston of 22 years ago was a very different animal. But whereas I had come to rely upon these tactics to resolve all questions and problems, loving you has revealed their inadequacies. Instinctively I have just worked harder at it to retain some semblance of order, but I suspect by allowing myself to love you, the whole strategy is called in question.

Whether there is any alternative strategy possible for me is, I suppose, a basic point at issue.

For the first time, his letter was signed 'with much love, *David*'. Two days later, on 9 August, another letter arrived, enclosing the Wallingford poem, and written in a much more cheerful mood. This one was signed, as usual, 'Wilfrid'. By 11 August, the issue was out in the open, and the letter was signed by both 'David' and 'Wilfrid', with a postscript by the dominant 'Wilfrid'. On the 14th, the signature was 'Wilfridavid' and by the 22nd it was simply 'David'. But, the battle was not over yet: on the 27th and 29th it was 'Wilfrid' again. 'David', however, held the field for most of September, except for the 21st when there was a solitary resurgence of 'Wilfrid'. What was all this about? It unfolded, step by step, in the letters themselves.

In his letter of 11 August, he referred to the 'desolation' of his return to the abbey after Wallingford, of 'knowing for the first time the bleak and bankrupt condition to which I had grown accustomed'. This mood, which had come over so strongly in the 6 August letter, was a combination of his heightened sense of difficulties within the community, to which he had previously been numbed, and his awareness of 'the Princess still sleeping and inaccessible'. My own Wallingford letter had reached him and partially reassured him of my love, but he was still troubled:

11 August 1981

You have enabled me to establish a real harmony between David and Wilfrid (roughly the 'affectionate' and the 'spiritual'), hence the importance to me of the 'religious' poems (now a past phrase). But there remains a more complex and problematic 'persona', with the mask of my office and role, which is less easily tamed.

Because of his abbatial persona he was insistent that our next meeting should not take place at the abbey (even if it was convenient in terms of distance), because he knew how 'disastrously artificial' he would be in that role: 'I will not say that I could not cope; the awful thing is that I could cope, by the inhumanity that is always so ready to hand.'

It did not seem to me that a 'real harmony' had yet been established between David and Wilfrid if he could write in such terms, but he reiterated his belief later in the letter: 'I do feel that the very earthy and human love (typified by David) is authenticated and validated by the Wilfrid who seemed to threaten any such human emotion in the past.' He closed the letter, which also contained dates and times for our next meeting, with the words: 'I fear all this must be a desperate bore for you. Genuine love should, surely, not need so much analysis and explanation. However, I think I love you; I think I love you unreservedly. Wilfrid. I *do* love you very much, David.' A postscript, signed by Wilfrid, merely said that probably all the foregoing should have been scrapped, but had been retained in deference to my desire to have his spontaneous thoughts and feelings.

By 14 August he was back in an uncomplicated mood of anticipatory 'joy and delight'. We were to meet five days later, and he was insistent that the whole day should be conducted in a mood of celebration:

14 August 1981

> There is your job to celebrate, also your next birthday proleptically (?!), and all your other birthdays retrospectively! Also I shall be celebrating 'The Year', which began with the Vauxhall week and, I think, symbolically ends as you begin your job, and I begin to set my sights on 1982. I want to consider this 'year' with gratitude, for all it has meant to me, meeting you, and getting to know you a little, and loving you and learning from you.
>
> As for the future, I will not consider it. You will perhaps be exploring the head-waters of the Limpopo River; I will be ploughing my furrow, sowing either wheat or tares . . .
>
> . . . I enclose something towards the expenses of the day in case you envisage any anticipatory purchase of petrol or provender. I shall have seen you three times in eight weeks; you are in danger of becoming a habit! Or would have been.
>
> With much love, prayers and anticipatory joy,
>
> Wilfridavid

By this time, I had found a job in the warehouse of the Oxfam Trading Company in Bicester, as a 'picker'. Not to be confused with a 'packer', the job entailed 'picking' the items on an order-sheet off the shelves and carrying them to a conveyor belt, which would transport them to the packers' department for dispatch. It was a hard, physical job (many of the items were heavy and high up), and mind-crunchingly boring, but it was what I needed just then: a routine that kept me occupied, but was totally without pressure or responsibility. The management was benevolent, and the women working there were full of humour and warmth, and came from many different walks of life. No questions were asked, and a real camaraderie soon developed between us, to the accompaniment of Radio 1 and frequent tea-breaks! I attempted to tell Wilfrid/David about it, but soon gave up, as it was such an alien world to him.

Wednesday, 19 August, was the day I finally fell in love with my whole heart. We spent the afternoon on the river again, but then decided on impulse to catch the train to London instead of going home. While we were there we went to a West End musical – *Pal Joey*, I think – but left in the interval (something I have never done before or since) because we were so conscious of time slipping away.

We found a pavement café and sat opposite each other, drinking coffee and looking into each other's eyes. For me it was the first time since Vauxhall that my stomach had really turned over with love for him. And it was all to do with me having backache! I remember sitting on a seat in Trafalgar Square (before the show) and watching him negotiate the crowds and the pigeons, in search of a cup of coffee for me from a sandwich stall. There was something new in his tenderness towards me, something physical in his protectiveness, which was all due to the backache. Never had I been so grateful for a physical pain!

He left me at the station and went off to catch his night-train to Edinburgh (he was going to stay with his brother). I waited, starry-eyed, for my train, only to discover that I had missed the last connection to Newbury. I rang my father, who agreed to meet the train to Reading, grumbling good-naturedly at my incompetence, but I don't remember minding one little bit for myself. It even seemed romantic being stranded on Reading station at midnight!

I am conscious of not writing 'Wilfrid' in the above account, because it seems to have been an experience that belongs to the relationship we now have, and the man I know now is David. As if in accord with this realization, his letter following our day in London was signed David, and was full of the same sense of a change in gear that I had felt:

22 August 1981

My dear,

Thank you for a wonderful, celebratory day. It is hard to believe that so much was packed into it.

I do hope that your return journey was not too problematic. I did feel badly about not having checked initially what the return trains were: it never occurred to me that last trains could be so early! Your mother will have an even dimmer view of this David character, but my main concern is that the ending of the day should not have seemed to have spoiled all that had gone before.

For me, the river with you, the picnic, the train journey to London, the West End and theatre, our 'parisien' tête à tête, and the journey back to Paddington, all had their perfections which nothing could spoil or detract from.

I was very concerned about your backache, but that made you seem the more dear and my feelings for you the more tender. I wish that I had been able to accompany you back to Newbury to know that you did get home safely and happily.

It was the first time for me in our recent meetings that our relationship had seemed completely real. I remember telling Rosemary around that time that I was getting seriously involved with him. She was not happy about it – partly, I think, because she knew more than anybody the pain I had experienced from my own time in community, and here I was going back to the 'scene of the crime'. Also, I think she was shocked at the thought of an abbot being involved in any kind of a love-relationship with a woman.

My mother, as David intimated in his letter, took a dim view of the relationship, from the point of view that she wanted me out of the influence of the religious life and into an independent life and career of my own. She too knew that it would almost certainly cause me more pain, though she was careful how she phrased her objection.

For my part, having now 'awoken' to love, I was much more aware of the precariousness of it and the likelihood of loss. I wrote to him for reassurance and received this letter in reply:

27 August 1981

> Your letter moved me deeply and I really do not know what to say! Has the Princess woken only to discover a sad, hard and empty world?
>
> . . . Think of my love for you as a strong and steady pulse of a life yet to be revealed. What shall be is less important than the reality of what is, and we must not allow uncertainties about the future to destroy our present.

His letter was written in the midst of a busy day in his office, with many interruptions and distractions, but ended nevertheless on a high note of hope:

> I will write again when I have written all that must be written, heard all that must be heard, said all that must be said. In all this I feel strengthened by my love for you, and your love for me; by accepting all this in truth, I can wait in hope for what shall be.
>
> With my gratitude and prayers and all my love.

> [Wilfrid]

Two things were new in this letter: one was his belief in my love for him, the other was that Wilfrid had written 'all my love'. I began to hope that somehow, by some miracle, we might find a way to be together permanently.

6
David Does Battle with Wilfrid

I had now moved back to Oxford and was again staying with Rosemary in her flat. She was very long-suffering about my smelly socks and my irritating habit of dumping used tea-bags in her enamel sink! Once my new job started, though, I pleasantly surprised her by bringing her tea in bed every morning. Yet it all seemed a far cry from Wilfrid/David's lonely resolutions in his cell-like office.

On the one hand, his latest poem, dated 29 August, was full of the pain that was sure to ensue when he had to give me up:

29 August 1981

Love is content to wait a hundred, a 1000 years
it is not content to wait for 'never'!
Better, surely, not to have loved, than to have loved and lost.

On the other hand, he could write just a few days later of a 'significant shift' in his attitude to things in the community:

Somehow I feel freed in respect of many things, some of them going back seven years, and others much longer. This is not only an internal feeling, but has allowed me to adopt and express a new policy which, although on a certain level more 'risky', is, I believe, more positive and creative. I have sketched this out to Chapter [all the professed monks in council], relating it to a three-year period, and it was surprisingly well received. I still love you too selfishly to be totally detached from the outcome, in the sense that I long for there to be some totally improbable miracle to set me free, but it does mean that I can perceive now how the love of you can work creatively not only in me but also in the situation in which I find myself, and that is really rather important if we are to go forward in the way of truth and integrity.

His letter of 12 September explained the idea behind the three-year period he had suggested to the monks. It seemed that he regarded that as a stage at which he could 'respectably resign as abbot'. Perhaps with this plan at the back of his mind, he began speculating on the Prince and Princess imagery again, stating firmly that soon I would have found the Prince of my dreams and his task would be over. And besides:

> I know that I cannot present a threadbare fellow like myself as the Prince, because my outward poverty conceals no hidden riches or unclaimed inheritance. It would seem presumptuous for me to propose any alternative without knowing your mind much more fully.

My birthday was now imminent (having been celebrated once already in anticipation on our 'London' day), and I was deluged with three letters, a card from the Tate gallery (he was in London visiting a female religious community) and two phone calls. My journal records my reaction:

18 September 1981

> Wilfrid phoned – twice. The second time to ask my forgiveness that his reply to my question of whether he loved me had not been sufficiently strong!
> I feel quite overwhelmed by this inloveness, by the amazing congruity of my preference and his response. His wit, his reserve, his lovely, austere courtesy, his impatience with himself. He called himself David over the phone when he introduced himself. I think now he could accept me in my jeans, humour me and still love me with the tenderness I crave. Perhaps there will be room to expand – *fully* – at last. Oh, I love him so much.

I conveyed something of this reaction to him in my next letter, and he picked out one image that particularly appealed to him. I had written, 'Maybe we will just grow old and mellow together, like two old apples.' His response to the image was that it 'cut away all the agonizing about *how* it would be', and allowed him 'just to relax, into the thought that it *would* be'.

He told me he was thinking of putting some of his new insights about the meaning of monastic life into written form. It made me feel rather peculiar to realize that this 'apple harvest' of ours might well be eventually used as compost, to fertilize the soil for a new blossoming of the religious life, but it filled him with great enthusiasm:

I feel strongly that the religious life is bogged down in the preparatory ascetic stage, making practical use of the communal discipline that results, without understanding that that is intended only to clear the ground for growth into love ('theosis') and the wholeness which that alone can bring – the wholeness in love for which we were made.

In his letter, he freely admitted that these new insights had come from his love for me; but a little later, on 24 September, he was delivering an address to the sisters of my ex-community on this subject, and he could not of course publicly acknowledge his sources there. He seemed amused by the irony of their enthusiastic reception of his message of the key role of love in the renewal of a religious community! But I found the whole thing very hard to take lightly, because of my still painful sense that I had been dubbed a failure in their eyes, a subversive who could not submit to the necessary discipline.

At this time, a new, almost apocalyptic strain was beginning to enter Wilfrid's letters:

21 September 1981

On the way [into Maidenhead] I saw a man sweeping leaves on the pavement, and I felt so envious of him. How I wished I was a sweeper of leaves with no other ties or commitments, and that as a sweeper of leaves I was loved by you.

He seemed intent on letting go of his usual tight self control, and seeing what happened when his real self was allowed to surface. But what was his real self?

My attitude to community is not entirely disinterested! Ironically David is taking over the abbacy, which is an unforseen outcome of recent events. He says that over the weir is the quickest way down the river, with survival reckoned at about 50%. It is a new approach, and one not without its merits and attractions. Various things recently have reminded me of my responsibilities here and the ways in which people inside and outside the community have come to rely upon me. But so much of it, on my part, is play-acting, role-playing, outward show, fulfilling expectations, without real substance.

How good by contrast to sweep leaves, and do it well, but with no pretences, no pretensions. How good it would be, 'truly to seek God', as a real person, and not as a puppet on a string.

Writing out his daily timetable for me exacerbated his sense of being stuck on a meaningless treadmill:

I have just written out for you my timetable. I am appalled to see, presented so baldly, the fact that I usually spend about seven hours at my desk every day, which includes seeing people as well as writing and reading. One does not have to be alive to go through this routine; indeed it is better not to be . . . I rarely do anything that an adequate secretary, or a properly programmed computer, could not do better, apart from my questionable role as an ikon or symbol of certain values which are more in the eyes of the beholder than myself. For seven years I have faithfully pedalled this machine [as abbot], with the attempt to meet other people's expectations as the highest goal. If David really gets into the saddle, I have no idea where we may end up, but it is likely to be a bumpier ride!

We had, so far, been very lucky in our exchange of letters, as none of them had been intercepted, but early in October there was a heartstopping few days when one of his letters was left on the seat in a train at St Pancras. It was full of dates and times of visits to bishops and priests and communities, and contained his secret plans for a revolutionary Chapter meeting with the monks. It was also every inch a love letter. I know all this because I finally received it a few days later – kindly posted by someone on the train.

This event made us realize how precarious our private world was. Maybe David was dicing with death on purpose to force Wilfrid's hand, but the latter was increasingly feeling the impossibility of doing anything precipitously. His 'secret'

plans for the Chapter consisted of a meticulously detailed programme for gradual withdrawal and increasing democratiz-
ation, so that when he finally resigned, the shock to the
community would be minimized. Yet we were still talking of a
three-year plan. It hardly seemed revolutionary to me.

In fact, the prospect of enduring so long in a role that was
increasingly suffocating him was making him feel old and
tired himself:

> Not the least of the difficulties is that Wilfrid seems to be an
> old man lacking energy or enterprise, and if I ever break
> away from here, the only justification would be if I did not
> again place myself in a position where the expectation of
> others imposed such unreal burdens.

The trouble was that when he thought of a future elsewhere,
he could not see what he would do. He was only trained to be
a priest, but he didn't want to put himself under the yoke of
people's expectations again. Any alternative would require
that very energy and enterprise that he could feel draining
away the longer he stayed. This 'general debilitated state' also
made him feel that he would be a burden on me, holding me
back from the bright future he seemed to envisage for me.

At this stage, I was waiting to go to my ACCM selection
board to see if I could do a deaconess training, and he was
determined not to be 'weakly dependent' on me. He wrote:
'Either I must muddle on here or else break away in some
positive way, in which I can recapture my strength and energy.'
It was becoming clear that his three-year plan did in fact have a
'secret' side. The Chapter meeting on 29 October was intended
to put the new systems and offices in place, so that he could
quietly fade away from the scene in a lot less than three years.

He had fixed no engagements for himself after October 1982,
and was quietly intending to push through his resignation
then. Once the resignation was achieved, he saw it only as a
question of 'gravitating towards the brink' until he 'disappeared over the edge'. He didn't seem to be able to think
beyond going over the edge, and his letters were increasingly
full of images of illness, dismemberment and death.

By this time, his community were beginning to pick up that
all was not well with him, commenting that he was 'unwell' or

'depressed', and he did not contradict their impressions. However, he was concerned that I should not hear rumours and be worried for him:

> In the unlikely event that you hear on some grapevine that I am unwell, do not worry, because as long as I am allowed to love you all is well, and if, incredibly, you should continue to love me, all is indestructibly well. The abbot and Wilfrid is ailing, and perhaps close to death, but that husk must die, that David, deep in the darkness of the life-giving earth, may put down some roots, and in due course throw up a shoot into the light of day.

I was both moved and appalled by these apocalyptic words. With all my heart I longed to be with him to help him emerge unscathed from the nightmare that his life had become, but I was daunted by the scale of the dissolution that was taking place within his psyche. It was as if he was encouraging part of his own flesh to wither and die, and was dancing on the funeral pyre without any thought that it was his own.

In my letters and over the phone, I did all I could to comfort and support him, but inside I still felt so raw and weak myself that I wasn't sure if I could keep us both afloat. It was around this time we had a very brief meeting, which clearly showed how close to the wind Wilfrid was sailing. He was in Dorchester for the Diocesan Synod, and the place was teeming with priests and religious lay people. Yet he suggested I meet him there and drive him to Reading for his train, so that we could have an hour or two together.

I parked in a big car park among a plethora of priestly vehicles, and waited for his arrival. He had promised to appear promptly, and he had just had time to sprint to the car and pull his habit over his head before we were surrounded by the black-suited multitudes. They were like ravens flocking around us, but Wilfrid kept his head down and we were soon out on the country roads. All I remember of that drive is a sort of quiet desperation.

As he waited for the Chapter meeting on the 29th, he seemed in a sort of limbo state, aware of the impossibility of going on as abbot, but also knowing the grave responsibilities he bore not to 'undermine anyone else's life'. He seemed to want to clarify and separate his private and public roles, and to this end had moved into a cell that was separate from his office, so that outside office hours he could have some privacy, and not sleep in the same place that he worked. He had furnished it very sparsely and very carefully – as if stripped for action. He wrote:

24 October 1981

> My new room is quite large by ordinary standards – perhaps 14 feet by 14 feet, with one rather small window, disproportionately small in relation to the wall area. . . . The furnishing is pleasantly plain, a narrow iron bedstead, simple desk, chest of drawers, bookcase, wooden armchair. All of it is simple and honest and true. My books are all hardback, which ought not to be significant, but somehow it is. Were it not for you I would know myself on the brink of another ascetic ego-trip, as in my novitiate days, but knowing you I know how sterile and negative and life-denying and pointless that all was . . .

By this stage, he was considering the implications not only of ceasing to be abbot, but of ceasing to be a monk; but to the Chapter, when it came, he outlined only his original plan of retiring after a three-year period. Ironically, the only things that were contested by the monks were the appointments of sub-prior and novice-master, both of which were intended as a means of decentralizing and democratizing his own power-base:

1 November 1981

> Life has been fairly lively since [the Chapter] as one after another of the community come to express their objections and complaints, or to hand out gratuitous advice! Today I detect a new reaction in myself which is not easily stirred. When I get really vexed, which is seldom, I become quietly resolute, and I can feel this taking over.

The monks were evidently not going to co-operate. So much for a smooth period of transition. But Wilfrid was quietly laying his plans for October 1982, ensuring that they had another religious superior on hand (in the guise of retreat conductor for the annual community retreat) for when he dropped his bombshell.

I very much needed to know what all these secret plans of his meant for us. Were we now talking of some definite decision being made for October 1982? Did it mean he intended to leave? At a gut level, I wanted him to make a snap decision so that I could plan my life accordingly. At an intellectual level, I knew we were in for a long period of reactions and reverberations while David and Wilfrid slogged it out. He wrote on 1 November:

1 November 1981

> Since Sunday afternoon I have been in a strange mood – partly an irrational elation, as though some great load had been removed; so at 'talking' meals over All Saints, Father Prior and Dom A. have had to contend with my quirky humour and repartee instead of the rather aloof silence to which they had become accustomed . . . I shall continue to act with my accustomed care and circumspection over the coming months, but deep down there is a sense of relief, release and even elation, as the burdens of a decade or two loosen their hold and fall away.

But community life carried on in its inexorable way; nothing changed, though the tensions within the structure increased as a result of the hostility stemming from the two new appointments.

One of the ironical observations David made at this time (he had now signed himself 'David' continuously for well over a month) was how much his sense of the inner meaning of monasticism had been sharpened by his 'conversion' to loving:

3 November 1981

> It struck me that if I were to leave here it would be more like Antony leaving his town for the desert than anything I had ever done! To go apart from society to seek God seems more fulfilled by leaving than by staying. I can hardly equate this place with 'corrupt society', but somehow for me it is as redolent of death as 'the cities of the plain'.

Yet he was still far from free of the web of responsibilities and duties and guilts that he had imposed upon himself, and his mood veered from elation to despair almost with every communication, though he did seem able to say on 8 November that at some level the decision was irrevocable: 'the resignation issue seems no longer my decision, as though some deeper subconscious level has determined it, and some large switch will be put to off when the time comes'. His main fear continued to be that by acting too precipitously he would wreak havoc both in his own community and the larger community of Anglican religious life. Yet he couldn't bear to stay for long in a place where he felt so alienated. My love, he said, was the source of what inner strength he had.

At the same time, he was conscious of talking too much, agonizing too much, in his letters, and could be quite amusing on the subject:

8 November 1981

You see the hazards of loving a reticent person who has the accumulated conversation of decades stacked away, mildewed and cobwebbed with disuse. Worse, I have an awful suspicion that tucked away in me there is also a factory all poised to turn out new mildewed and cobwebbed conversation . . . !

The weekend after this letter, we met – in the agonizingly public setting of the reception area of Nashdom Abbey – and I was hard put to match him in the brevity and impersonality of his conversation. It was a post-Vauxhall meeting, and the young monk who had called it knew us both well. I know, with hindsight, that nobody guessed anything, though David admitted to blushing when it was first mentioned I would be there. I cannot now remember why I didn't tell him myself – probably I was desperate to see him and guessed he might well absent himself through caution if forewarned.

We had barely a minute or two alone, but the poignancy of being together, unable to speak, was sweet in itself. However, the following weekend we had a proper 'life' organized: nine hours together in Oxford. As a keepsake, at the end of the day, I gave him my own much thumbed copy of Laurence

Whistler's poems *To Celebrate Her Living*, a companion volume to *Initials in the Heart*. I had inscribed in the flyleaf a line from one of the poems that meant a lot to me, and over the next few weeks it came to haunt David too. The line was 'some whole for which dividedness was made', and it came from a poem called 'To the Centre'.

David was delighted, though I have little doubt that the poems must have heightened his sense of the gap between what he longed for and what he actually had to endure. That November, he wrote to me about the election of a new abbess in one of the Benedictine orders he was closely involved with:

> It was the sort of outside occasion at which I am most aware of the expectations of others concerning me. It is, of course, only a fragment of the total picture, but it makes me aware of how important it is when there is an amputation to tie off the arteries and cauterize the wound if the patient is to live.

But his resolve was unweakened: 'meanwhile I cling to that vision which you have revealed to me of that whole for which dividedness was made. Ultimately I cannot bolster up a system and a situation which is so alien from my own new perception of the truth.'

My own situation was on the verge of being transformed by the offer of a country cottage – rent free – just outside Oxford. It would resolve all our problems about meeting, and take the onus off Rosemary, who was still uneasy about our relationship, yet obliged to be host to our occasional meetings. David was thrilled, though sympathetic when I told him of my feelings of insecurity about leaving the safe haven of Rosemary's flat.

The person who owned the cottage was a friend of a friend, who seemed grateful to have it occupied over the winter months until she could move in herself. I was paid such a basic wage at the warehouse that I could never have afforded a proper rent, so we were both pleased with the arrangement. The cottage was in a place called Bletchingdon, a very attractive Cotswolds village, which also had the benefit of being nearer to my job at Bicester. As a result, I could get up a little later for my 8.30 a.m. start at the warehouse – though anything seemed an indulgence after five years of getting up at 5.30 a.m.!

On 24 November David arranged a complicated manoeuvre: to give me his clock radio to take with me to the cottage. We met for about 40 minutes at Rosemary's flat, in between two of his other engagements in Oxford. Rosemary was there and David felt 'closely chaperoned', but the effect was to reassure him that the bond between us was so well established that communication was possible on a deep level even if the conversation was superficial. He was also reassured that he could appear in his Wilfrid persona and still feel as David. For myself, I felt rather more torn, as silent communication was also possible on a deep level between myself and Rosemary – and I felt her unease.

His engagement after seeing me was at All Saints again, and he was suddenly conscious that my scent hung about him in a way that those who knew me might detect. I don't know if he meant a particular perfume or a personal scent; if the former, it would be unlikely to ring any alarm bells, because we were never allowed to wear any perfume in community and therefore none would be associated with me. However, according to his letter of the following day: 'the scent persisted throughout the journey back and during supper, especially on my left hand. Before recreation I washed it away, not being sure how pervasive it might be.' After Compline, he also found himself abstractedly collecting a few strands of my hair from his scapular, and pressing them between the pages of *To Celebrate Her Living*.

It made us both realize how little we had allowed for the evidence of the other three senses in concentrating on not giving ourselves away through look and speech. In community, such things were minutely observed. I remember recognizing 'Tweed' perfume on a guest at 50 paces when I was in the convent – all the way from one end of the choir to the other end of the nave!

7
Snow

I moved into the cottage at the end of November 1981, at the start of a cold spell that was to last two months – with snow both in December and January. I loved the cottage, but it was very cold. It was heated by storage heaters that were only lukewarm in the evening, and there must have been something wrong with the chimney, or the size of the grate, because even with a good fire going I had to sit with my coat and gloves on and my feet on the fender!

I don't know if the cold contributed to it, or if it was caused by my job, but I spent the first week in the cottage nursing an extremely painful shoulder. David was very solicitous about it, and quite dispersed my fears that he wouldn't be able to cope with mere physical problems. He wrote:

> I must say how concerned I am that you have been in such pain. I do hope that you will take care that the work is not too heavy and that you allow yourself time to mend. You are altogether too precious to be hurt by any job, however great the rewards, let alone by the one which you are doing. You almost encourage me to do something really dramatic and come and look after you NOW!

For his birthday on 8 December, I sent him a copy of Dorothy Sayers's *Busman's Honeymoon*. Partly I was intrigued to see if he made any link between himself and Peter Wimsey, and partly I wanted him to read a book with a supremely happy ending for a change! (The book is about the honeymoon of Peter Wimsey and Harriet Vane, achieved after many trials and setbacks.) But I inadvertently upset him by saying how much it mattered to me that he should like it: 'I have to confess that, foolishly, a cold stab of fear went through me when you jokingly said that if I do not like the book you are sending, "it's all off". The words seemed to be so easily said . . . and so final.'

I had meant him to see how much our relationship had in common with theirs: she prickly and independent, he devoted and sensitive, but it had only mattered in that sense, nothing more portentous. He admitted on this occasion that he was hypersensitive as to whether I would stop loving him once I really knew him.

His mind, as ever, was running in at least two ways at once. On the one hand, he was speculating about how he would react and feel if he did in fact leave the community in a year. On the other, he was convinced that his resignation from the abbacy and his dispensation from his vows as a monk would have to be separated in time, in order to prevent an explosive reaction in the religious world: 'There would be a certain simplicity and economy in taking both together but that seems a more destructive policy. Out of the limelight, I can more easily handle the really difficult stage.'

My own reaction to this was a kind of despair at the interminable time it was all going to take, particularly as we now seemed to be going backwards again; any prospect of 'normal' happiness seemed to be receding into the future at a rate of knots. I tried to be supportive, but my own experience of leaving community had been so different, so explosive and sudden, and so uncomplicated by duties and responsibilities that I found it hard to be in tune with his necessary caution and secretiveness. I admitted my feelings on the phone that December, and immediately wished I hadn't because it plunged him into such a despairing mood that I was overcome with guilt. He wrote, on his birthday of all days:

8 December 1981

Perhaps the sensible thing is for you to proceed as though I do not exist, free to range across the map unhampered, and then see what might become possible and acceptable. I do realize how different the circumstances are for you, and your proper impatience at my laboured progress.

I can understand your desire to be loved more robustly, more immediately, more effectively. One can envisage many circumstances in which it would be a joy to drop everything on impulse, and come to you. But somehow these do not seem to be my circumstances. Ironically it is from you that I have most fully learnt the meaning of truth and integrity, but they only serve, it seems, to purify the qualities of duty and responsibility, not negate them.

It was snowing heavily at the time, and his sense of possible loss and rejection seemed to have got all mixed up with the freezing conditions and the isolation caused when the telephone lines came down:

> It is no ordinary snow,
> it epitomizes the frozen, icy grip of winter,
> closing ever tighter upon the earth and trees,
> from which the life drains.
>
> Not everything shall live to see the spring,
> For some things, the circle of life has ended,
> for others, although in expectation of longer life,
> the cold will prove too severe . . .

But then my letter finally arrived – after nine days of silence – and the deathly snow images began to change to muted images of Varykino and the snow-bound idyll of Yuri and Lara, celebrated in *Dr Zhivago* (a book that he had read five times.) He was also finding (to his great relief!) a great affinity in himself to the mood and characters of *Busman's Honeymoon*, and it soon entered our pantheon of significant allegories.

By now, he had decided to tell his brother Frank about us, as he was considering a move down into the Oxford diocese from Edinburgh, where he was principal of a theological college. David was concerned as to how he might react, in case any scandal reflected back on his brother.

Meanwhile, I was trying to persuade him to come and meet my family over Christmas, when we were all gathered together in a rented house in Herefordshire. He was dubious about the plan – no doubt rightly so – though at the time I was very disappointed. In the event, Christmas passed without any contact between us, except by phone. My family still thought it all rather odd, but at least David didn't have to experience their incredulity.

Our next meeting took place in the first week of January in quintessentially 'Zhivagoesque' conditions. It had been snowing hard for several days and I had had to dig my car out in the mornings with a shovel. Driving to work had been a case of using the car like a sledge and sliding down the hill to the main road! I was very proud of the little car, as it had started every morning (despite the lack of a garage) and I had not missed a single day at work. Fleur had been equally intrepid – bundled up in a blanket on the passenger seat while I was in the warehouse, and going for her walk at lunchtime in drifts above her ears!

That particular Saturday, the weather had really closed in, but I was determined to get to David, who was in retreat at the same enclosed community in Oxford where I had been in my last month before leaving. I set out towards Oxford in a half-light. The roads were deserted, for the blizzard was at full strength. The pavements were taken over by children revelling in the extremity of the conditions. As the car crawled up Iffley Road and I saw David, muffled up, trudging towards me through the murk, I could almost hear Lara's theme from *Dr Zhivago* striking up! An obscure line from one of D. H. Lawrence's poems kept running through my head: 'Look, we have come through!' I don't remember anything about the rest of that day – just the mood of our meeting.

However, I have forgotten to mention two important events that occurred before this memorable encounter: my introduction to Frank, and David's introduction to my parents. Both events passed without too much trauma at the end of the Christmas holidays, though we both felt like naughty children whose games were being judged by grown-ups from the real world of 'telegrams and consequences'.

Frank had come to the cottage with David, and I had made us all dinner, without any obvious culinary disasters. Frank had been charming and friendly, though it had taken a letter to David from Frank's wife Poppy to provide me with a more spontaneous reaction from them:

21 December 1981

You certainly did manage to take our breath away! When I read your letter I thought for an awful minute you were going over to the Pope or something (clearly a fate worse than death . . . !). Instead here was a much more productive outcome, a whole set of possibilities to which one can only say, three cheers, even if it means taking a deep breath and wondering how things can best be worked out. I hope you don't really think Frank or I are going to be shocked/ dismayed/disapproving. That would be quite the wrong tack . . . of course what matters is that you're really sure (equally, of course, one never is!), though you can't have had that much chance to discover. . . . Anyway I can't comment very helpfully at this stage, and I'm glad Frank will have a chance to come and talk after Christmas. But rest assured our sentiments are warm and supportive, with a touch of the wry amusement ('the cunning old thing . . .') at what these Westons get up to.

The meeting with my parents had rather more edge to it, though they both did their best to be welcoming and cordial. David particularly took to heart my mother's comment that he was going to get out 'just in time'. He was himself very aware that two years previously he would not have been receptive, and two years thence would have been too late! It strengthened his sense of providentiality, of the whole thing being part of God's plan, though I am not convinced my mother meant it in quite that sense!

On 21 and 22 January I had interviews at Westcott House Theological College in Cambridge where, much to my delight, I was given a place. It remained for me to get through the ACCM Selection Board four days later, so that I would have the necessary funding, as well as establishment approval for ordination as a deaconess. The three-day conference at Bristol was taxing but stimulating, and I enjoyed the group discussions and exercises. However, as soon as the individual interviews started, I was in trouble.

I tried hard to avoid controversial subjects such as the ordination of women, even though the question whether women could be ordained deacon was being debated in Synod at that time. I think I succeeded in presenting a suitably 'balanced' viewpoint, though they were very dubious about my desire to become a chaplain rather than a parish worker.

Everything was going all right until I unthinkingly asked the Secretary of ACCM whether the grant would still be payable to a married woman. He immediately wanted to know who I was going to marry and what sort of job he had. When I said a priest, he wanted to know where; and when I was rather reluctant to tell him, he pressed for an answer. Eventually, I was forced to admit he was a monk. Immediately, the tone changed. I was told I was a 'dangerous' woman in heavy chauvinist terms, and left in no doubt that things would go badly for me if I persisted in this course.

A letter duly arrived informing me that I had not been accepted. The reasons adduced were to do with experience and maturity, but I knew perfectly well what the real reason was. I was angry and upset, and had barely adjusted to this bombshell when David rang me up with another. The prior (his second in command) had died suddenly of a heart attack – in his presence. Apart from being upsetting in itself, this radically changed the picture for David, as there was now no obvious successor. It seemed horribly like a 'sign' and stopped him in his tracks. He wrote on 2 February 1982: 'I do affirm the providentiality of our meeting at Vauxhall, and of all that we have shared since, but it will require great sensitivity to find the way forward from here, and more trust and honesty than I possess alone.'

I had now to find the generosity to respond to this setback sympathetically when I already felt that my own career chances had been wrecked by reinvolvement with the wretched religious life. There was a tearful phone call with David, who didn't really understand why the ACCM episode had upset me so much, as he had always counselled me against re-entering the restricted confines of the church.

I felt desperate. Rosemary saved me by whisking me away for the weekend to a remote waterside inn in Symond's Yat, near Ross-on-Wye. It was a deeply restorative time of walking and talking, and experiencing her practical affection. I returned to the cottage able to face the next stage.

Things were changing on all sides. My tenancy of the cottage was approaching its end, and the job at the warehouse had suddenly finished (it had always been temporary). What was I to do next? Where was I to go?

In the short term, I was able to appreciate not getting up at seven every morning, and as I had the cottage at least till

March, I decided to use the time to do some work on the book I was writing about the religious life. David and I had been planning to meet at the cottage on St Valentine's Day, and there had even been talk of David staying the night there. In the light of all that had happened, though, he was suitably tentative: '2 February 1982: You might consider it inappropriate in our present state of uncertainty, and I would certainly not want to make things more painful and difficult for the future, whatever it may be.'

Yet the need to talk things over remained, so plans were laid for the 14th.

He had looked up the word 'dangerous' for me in *The Initials in the Heart*, as he was sure that Laurence Whistler had applied it very positively to Jill. Although unable to find the exact reference he had been looking for, he sent this quotation from Chapter XII:

> She was gay and darkling, flame-like, yet demure; and somehow contrived to be 'dangerous', in two senses, her own and the medieval simultaneously.

I wasn't sure what the medieval sense of 'dangerous' was, but it seemed exotic rather than negative, and I felt better.

At this time, David had been sorting through the prior's voluminous papers, and was feeling oppressed by the sense of waste, of a 'life drained away into all that useless effort and energy'. Yet he realized even as he said it that he was really talking about his own reaction to the religious life, and the crushing prospect of going on with no end in sight. He continued to have a full timetable of meetings and visits in his capacity as Confessor and Chaplain General to several female religious communities, but these visits were infinitely easier to him than 'simple' tasks within his own community – such as professing novices. Here he was only too conscious that his heart was elsewhere.

Yet there was no way out that he could initiate for himself; his sense of duty was absolute. All he could do was to pare down his papers and belongings and take on no new engagements – as if he had 'been given nine months to live'. He wrote on 7 February 1982, 'It is not very much, but it is the most I can actively do just now to feed some discontinuity into the system.' He kept hoping that something momentous would come from outside and force a showdown: 'I feel that I need an explosion, without myself having pressed the plunger.'

The great schemes for the 14th didn't work out quite as planned, as my car broke down, and we had to stay in the vicinity of the cottage instead of making an expedition to the South Downs where David's father had been rector of a parish at the time of his death. Yet the great thing was that we had *time* together – not the usual 'brief life', but an immensely long day and a night. We walked and talked in the spring sunshine, and then, as David expressed it later in his letter, 'the evening stretched ahead with no threat of leave-talking to fret the edges of joy'.

My memory of the day is more ambivalent. The fact that the car had 'turned against me' made me feel ridiculously insecure, and it wasn't helped by the fact that I was still waiting to be 'processed' by the DHSS, although I had been laid off from work for a week or so by now. I had also been very shaken by David's change of heart after the prior's death, and couldn't help but be full of anger at the hold that the religious life still held over *my* life, through my love for David. I wanted to cut loose and make my own life: perhaps go to Africa – anywhere, as long as I could be moving, and not just hanging around waiting.

As a result, I was restless all that day, impatient with David's delight in small pleasures of the moment, wanting to puncture his romantic sentiments, yet all the time needing his love so much. How could he be content with so little? How could he bear the artificiality of sleeping in the same house, but not together? Yet at the same time I was also frightened of intimacy. Because of all this, I was genuinely surprised when his letter describing the day arrived a few days later, for he seemed so content. Perhaps he really had mastered the monastic principle of living in the present moment.

It was the beginning of Lent, and I went again to Nashdom Abbey. I knew I wanted to see David in his abbatial role, as he was so much the perfect monk on the outside that there was a real beauty and pathos in his bearing. Then there was the secret joy of seeing him there in his remoteness and inviolability, and knowing he was 'mine' in spirit. But it was moving to receive communion from his hands, and the seriousness of that sacrament prevented my schoolgirlish excitement from getting out of hand.

Later on, a group of us stood in the hall having coffee, and David gave me directions to get back to my parents' house (where I was staying). It was a public conversation, but, as before, it held much private meaning for both of us. Judging by subsequent letters, we went undetected – even by the most astute of female observers.

In his letter of 25 February, David made it clear that despite the prior's death, he was back to thoughts of leaving. He had also had further thoughts about the David/Wilfrid split. The aspect that was worrying him now was the conviction that the Wilfrid persona had been merely grafted on to the 22-year-old David, and that when it was finally rejected, the man who emerged would be immature and intellectually stunted for his age. Not surprisingly, this worried him.

He became aware that he was 'increasingly resolved to resign' in October of that year (1982), whatever the difficulties; but he was also appalled by the prospect of how bleak life would be within or without the community if he encouraged me to develop a life independent of him, which his conscience urged him to do: 'to leave and be without you is probably just to jump out of the refrigerator into the "deep freeze" '. I wanted to reassure him that it would be all right, but I myself was slightly appalled by the thought that his happiness depended so much on me, when my own emotional life was so volatile. It was like reassuring a 22-year-old, when I wanted to be able to discuss the pros and cons with a wise 44-year-old.

Yet one heartening note in his letter at the end of February was the discovery from one of the junior monks who was close to him that the community was still actively speculating about his possible resignation and even suggesting successors. This was news indeed!

However, another kind of news reached me during this time that obliterated everything else for a while. One of my closest friends from community days, Sister Ben, who had first introduced me to the convent, was discovered to have inoperable stomach cancer.

I went to see her in hospital after the results of her explora-
tory operation, and we joked and talked in our usual off-hand
but affectionate way. For some reason, which made me feel
deeply touched, she wanted me to be the one who went with
her on her convalescence at a retreat house in Wales. I knew
that she wanted to be with someone who would just take all
the 'God-business' for granted, and we had always been able
to do that. So I dropped everything and packed my bags. We
planned to be there for a fortnight beginning on 8 March, and
looked forward to the company of the three liberated sisters
there, and the beauty and tranquillity of the setting in the
Brecon Beacons.

March was a very busy month for David as there were celebrations within the community – a diamond jubilee of vows
and a profession – and duties outside, which included a difficult visit to one of the female Benedictine communities where
he had to initiate a critical examination of the constitution. His
letter of 14 March 1982 told me his timetable for the month,
and it seemed that his duties and my time away with Sister
Ben meant that we would probably not see each other before
Holy Week. I planned to go to the abbey for Maundy Thursday – drawn again by the desire to see him and the chance of
participating in one of my favourite liturgies.

David knew Sister Ben a little himself and wrote the following: 'Although you are bound to feel distress for Sister B, I
hope that it will also be a time of joy for you, knowing that you
are the person that she wants to be with at such a time.' He
then referred to the issue that I knew was bound to come up in
my two weeks alone with Sister Ben: should I tell her about us?

You seemed to conclude that it would be wiser not to say
anything to her about us, and that is consistent with my own
instinct, but I would want to leave you free to speak as
seems best. In such circumstances conversation might be on
such a level that one could not have envisaged.

Such, of course, proved to be the case. We had a wonderful
time together – only heightened by the knowledge that she
was under a suspended death sentence. Each day she managed to walk a little further down the lane, and we both enjoyed the comical behaviour of Fleur, who was wild about the

rabbits she kept detecting in the woods on either side of the lane.

We didn't talk much about death as we were both optimists by nature, but used the time instead to talk about ourselves and our lives. Sister Ben was then in her sixties, and had lived a very full and exciting life before entering the community when she was over forty. She had been a literary agent, and had known many famous writers and celebrities of the post-war period.

There had also been a man that she had loved passionately: and although she had been in the convent nearly twenty years and had led a richly varied and fulfilling life there, she still felt anger and loss when she talked about him. He had recently died, and had made no attempt to contact her in his final illness.

All this gradually came out in the dark evenings as we sat around the fire in our small chalet; and there was a sense of her rounding her life off, searching for the pattern. It seemed impossible not to reciprocate, and to tell her my most cherished dreams. In her characteristic way, she was not in the least shocked, but entered into the secret with conspiratorial glee. We conceived a plan that we were convinced would overcome all the obstacles, get David out, and get us together.

8

The Welsh Solution

Not far from where we were staying, there was a retreat house cum smallholding cum mini-community that Sister Ben was involved with, and knew was on the look-out for some additional, sympathetic members. The plan was that I should go to St Gregory's and spend some months there as part of the community, and that David should get himself seconded there after his resignation as abbot. As it happened, the place was already affiliated to David's abbey, so there was a connection, and hence his action would not appear too strange.

Sister Ben and I felt it would be the ideal setting for him to wind down, as it had a chapel and regular Benedictine worship, but the atmosphere was also informal. There was much therapeutic manual work to be done on the smallholding – tending the pigs, ducks and vegetables – and, above all, it was run by a family with children, as well as other single people.

The only stumbling block was that there would be the possibility of some scandal adhering to the community when it became known that David was not planning to go back to the abbey, but leaving to get married. Also, of course, there was always the possibility that the members themselves might not want us. With characteristic bravado, Sister Ben and I brushed this possibility aside and set about laying our plans with great vigour and enthusiasm.

In the meantime, David had been fighting fierce internal battles within his own community. The 'younger' monks (40-year-olds) had been accusing him of allowing a gerontocracy to flourish at their expense, while the older ones questioned both his health and his competence in the face of the revolt from 'the new guard'. David had obviously felt rather mauled by these attacks, though ironically they made the prospect of resignation easier. I don't think I realized until I read the letter describing these battles (soon after I arrived in Wales) how hard his self-appointed task of reconciling the warring factions had been over the seven years of his abbacy.

He wrote on 10 March of how for once he had 'lost his cool' and allowed things to get to him, but at least there was a note of joy in it all:

10 March 1982

As I said last night [over the phone], the thought of you and your love is an inextinguishable flame of joy which burns unwaveringly in the darkness, making all things possible, and enabling me to see the humour and appreciate the irony of what otherwise would be unbearable.

His next letter was full of unconscious irony in that he spoke of a spontaneous visit from Brian O'Malley, the head of St Gregory's. Brian had responded so quickly to Sister Ben's suggestion that I visit them and possibly join them, that he had been to consult David about it – even before I had told him myself! Because I had not yet told David of the plan, he excused himself gracefully when Brian himself suggested that David might like to spend some months with them (Brian obviously knew nothing of the connection between us). David wrote:

I was able to give several authentic-sounding reasons for not being involved personally, although I must say it sounds delightful . . . If one were looking for community life with a difference I am sure that it has much to commend it. But, needless to say, it pales into total insignificance when set alongside the possibility of being with you.

I waited on tenterhooks for him to receive the letter that explained 'the plan', for he was away for several days visiting some of the communities he had mentioned in his earlier list of duties for March. At one community, he had been obliged to discuss the mechanics of release from vows and 'exclaustration' (extended leave of absence), and was relieved to discover that they held no terrors for him. There were daily letters from all the various places he was visiting, but still no response to the crucial letter, as he had not yet received it. I began to wonder if someone else intercepted his letters now the prior was dead, but he hadn't mentioned it.

One of his letters – ironically – spoke about how crucial it was for nobody to hear anything about me if his departure was to be without protracted opposition and pain, but still I heard nothing of 'the plan'. Then finally the letter came; it was so calmly cautious and dismissive that I felt winded by it:

> With regard to the retreat and the possibility of my going there, I would be interested to see it, but in view of their formal links with us, it would be hardly fair to them for me to use it as a place for formally deciding to sever my links with Nashdom. . . . St Gregory's is at a crucial stage of affiliation to Nashdom which I would not wish to damage.

One pararaph, and the discussion was over. The letter went on to express his delight that I was having such an 'inaustere Lent', and his own sense of new life that love had given to his 'atrophied and shrivelled-up heart'. Almost in spite of myself, I thought of the lovely line in George Herbert's poem 'The Flower':

> Who would have thought my shrivelled heart
> could have recovered greenness?

An alternative suggestion followed hard on mine, though. He had been talking to some friends and contacts in London who wanted Nashdom's backing to set up a Vauxhall-type community in west London. If he went there for a few months after his resignation, he knew he could put it to his own monks as an extension of their apostolate, and it would be a good transitional experience for him in learning to function 'outside' in a meaningful context, with friendly, supportive people around him. He said that I could be part of it if I wanted to, or I could do my psychotherapy course in London – part of a new plan conceived since the ACCM rejection. Either way – whether I was involved or not – he wouldn't be a burden on me.

In some ways this seemed an admirable alternative solution, so why didn't I respond positively to it? Partly, I was afraid of London: its vastness, noise and bustle, and also its dynamism. And at the same time it was true that I had fallen for St Gregory's – both the people and the place. Whatever my reasons, David sensed the 'lostness' in my voice when we exchanged schemes over the phone and he turned mine down. But by the next day (17 March), he was already moving towards 'the

Welsh solution' and his subsequent letters confirmed it. In the event, we decided to wait upon the result of my interview at the Westminster Pastoral Foundation in London regarding the psychotherapy course, before mentioning our joint decision to any of the key people.

Sister Ben and I returned to Oxford from Wales a few days earlier than planned, as she seemed so well and we both had things to attend to. A letter from David was awaiting me:

19 March 1982

> This letter is to welcome you back to the cottage, to tell you that I love you more and more, and to say that I have been feeling ecstatic since our phone conversation last night and your letter this morning. My main efforts today have been to try and keep a big smile off my face.
>
> Suddenly it all seems possible and credible. All the problems just seemed to fall away; it was like crossing rough country and feeling lost as one fights one's way through thickets, suddenly to emerge on a road with a signpost showing the destination to be close.

The arrangement with St Gregory's now stood on the basis that David and I were both going to go there for a time, though the members knew nothing of any connection between us. Brian had been alerted to the possibility that David might well leave Nashdom during his time in Wales, but no more. At the same time, my interview for the psychotherapy course was about to take place, and I travelled to London for it in some trepidation.

David wrote from the Male Superiors Conference on 23 March to wish me luck. They had been discussing monks and brothers who had left to get married, but had reacted with such a lack of comprehension that he had felt no impulse to share his own doubts and difficulties. It was significant that he felt no distress at the thought that next year they might be discussing his defection.

The course at the Westminster Foundation had a Jungian base, which attracted me very much after my own experience of psychotherapy. And as I assimilated my own sense of hurt at the ACCM rejection, I began to feel more drawn to working on the fringes of the church. David was right: I would feel too constricted within the structures again, but there was satisfying and exciting work to do as an 'involved outsider'. I knew I was still looking for a 'life's work' to which I could give all my displaced energy and enthusiasm. I also wanted a real qualification, which would provide independence in both financial and intellectual terms.

In the event, the interviews – both the group ones and the individual one – were far more gruelling than anything ACCM had thrown at me, but I was reasonably sure I had stood up under fire. What I wasn't sure about was whether I actually wanted to go there if there was that much hostility at just the interview stage. All the way home – first on the Underground, and then on the train – I struggled to identify some elusive sense of uneasiness that I felt about the place. I had experienced it at both sets of interviews, and it wasn't simply a product of the hostile interview technique. When I finally identified it – about Reading – I realised it was a species of the convent mentality which I could no longer tolerate. It went under the name of the 'we know you better than you know yourself' syndrome, and it underlay all their assumptions.

Yet by the time the train had reached Oxford I had decided that I could beat the system, and that if they offered me a place (unlikely), then I would accept it. In the event, I didn't have much time to worry about their response, as Hilary, an old school friend, rang me from Cheshire to take me up on an old offer to help her out with her children if things got too hectic during the setting up of her new business.

This meant abandoning the cottage, but the tenancy had nearly run out anyway; and as Wales was now set for August, things were looking very impermanent already. David and I were having long discussions over the phone about how we would fit everything in. Cheshire wasn't a problem; the real problem was how we would manage if I was accepted on the psychotherapy course and started just as he was on the brink of coming out of his community.

We finally came to the conclusion that if I *was* accepted, I would defer for a year to make it possible to be with David in Wales after his dispensation from his vows. Part of me was dubious about his decision not to have time on his own to work through his reactions to leaving, but my protective instincts jumped at the chance to be around when he most needed help. Too often I had had to suffer, and let him suffer, at a distance. Not again.

So I set off for Cheshire, knowing that the future was planned as far as was possible. It was, in any case, only a few weeks before Easter, and I was planning to spend at least some of Holy Week at Nashdom Abbey. David managed to snatch a few hours from his busy schedule to come and help me say goodbye to the cottage. It was a sunny farewell to a place where we had been happy, though I shall always remember it as the place where I had to sit in coat and gloves with my feet almost in the fire to keep warm!

There were two or three weeks before Easter for me to settle in in Cheshire, and for us to work out some sort of pattern for our days. Hilary had two young sons, so they moved in together into one bedroom and I had the other. One of the boys had just started school, but the younger one, Daniel, was only just over two, so he and I spent a lot of time together. I also did the housework and made the boys' meals, so that things were reasonably under control when Hilary and her husband came home from their bookshop.

There were tensions of course for all of us, mostly centring on the question of privacy. I was very aware of my own tenuous independent existence in contrast to the solidity and warmth of their family life. I found it difficult that they were both atheists, and couldn't help but regard my previous 'ivory tower existence' in the convent with deep incredulity.

Yet there were many compensations – one of them being the bond that developed between Fleur and Daniel. When his elder brother Ben went off to school, Daniel would still be dreamily eating his cereal in his pyjamas, and I would often catch him and Fleur relishing alternate spoonfuls to the strains of *Bridge over Troubled Water*, which was our joint favourite L.P.!

David's life in the monastery was even further removed from all this, though there were occasional incursions from the 'real' world in the form of weddings that he would officiate at for friends. In my first weeks in Cheshire he had to take a wedding for the daughter of a family friend, and this made him actively conscious of his own views on wedding ceremonies – particularly the sort he did not want to have for himself. He was oppressed by the number of guests, by the enormous cost, by the artificiality of the speeches, and by the absence of a Eucharist at the heart of the celebration. Afterwards, he wrote out for me what his own ideal wedding would be like: small, with only a few special guests, a beautiful church, and a Eucharist embedded like a jewel in a perfect musical setting. It all seemed like a remote and beautiful fantasy – almost like a defence to cover his own uneasiness about the prospect of taking another 'solemn vow' so soon after the necessary breaking of the first.

At this stage he still would not allow himself to think too far ahead, nor make any concrete plans. There were too many days to get through before October. I had been offered a place on the psychotherapy course, but was unable to raise the necessary money for the fees, so was back to square one with my career plans. We had seen each other two or three times over Easter, but our meetings were tantalizingly brief and public.

Everything was now geared to the prospect of David's imminent departure for the Holy Land, where he would assist with a pilgrimage as spiritual director. He wrote on 22 April: 'I have never been away with less pleasurable anticipation.' I too felt keenly that separation was a very different thing when we were talking of vast tracts of sea as well as land between us. In one of his last letters before departure he seemed to be suffering from a sudden failure of nerve, as if he could not really believe that there was a way out for him:

At points during today, and on most days, I have glimpses of the pain ahead and I wish I was more sure that I shall come through it well. You really ought not to feel too committed to me until you see how it works out. Sometimes I get a great hollow feeling inside – the opening of a sort of bottomless pit – and I wonder if that was how it was, what would then become of my fine words. It hits me at night sometimes, or when over-exposed to the ecclesiastical establishment. In that situation my instinct would be, I think, to go and hide. It sounds childish, but I suppose that one's responses to pain and distress tend to be very basic and unsophisticated . . .

He flew to Israel on 27 April, and I was soon flooded with a succession of postcards and letters, starting with one written on the flight out. In the event, he enjoyed his stay much more then he had anticipated, despite some rather menacing skirmishes between the Arabs and the Israelis in Jerusalem while they were staying there. Their trip also coincided with the Falklands War, and he said how strange it was to listen to the coverage on Jordanian television and realize that they identified with us in our fight to throw off the 'invader'. David's feelings towards the war were – like mine – ambivalent, to say the least.

Yet most of the trip was heavily devotional rather than political. There were daily Eucharists and 'stations' at all the biblical sites, with Bible readings and hymns that David was supposed to organize. The group were pleasant and friendly, but quite resistant to any 'stepping out of role' – so that he felt their embarrassment keenly on an excursion day when he wore 'secular' clothes to go swimming with them all! Normally, this incident wouldn't have mattered to him, but at the time it exacerbated his already painful sense of muddled identity.

Each night he kept himself going with a few pages of *Gaudy Night*, waiting for the happy ending between Harriet and Peter Wimsey that I had assured him would come. The sense of us as a couple was dim while he was so firmly fixed in his spiritual director role, but he also felt his ties with Nashdom loosened somewhat: 'It is odd to think I shall be at Nashdom the day after tomorrow. It has been a long enough absence to feel that some of the ties have been permanently cut, and that I need to keep it that way.'

Meanwhile, my time in Cheshire was nearing its end, and I was beginning to lay my plans for the coming months in more detail. I had arranged to go with Sister Ben to a retreat house in East Anglia run by Philippa's father, to help her conduct a silent retreat. We had done such a 'double act' before while I was in community, and knew that we functioned well together. That was to be in June, and after that I was having a brief holiday in the Lake District.

August was still the month set for my departure to Wales. The latest plan was for me to wait for David at St Gregory's until he had resigned, and then somehow or other he would join me there. We had not really worked out the logistics yet, but it seemed workable.

We managed to snatch two meetings on the Sunday and Tuesday after his return from Israel. On the Sunday I happened to be staying with my parents in Kintbury, and on the Tuesday he was up in Manchester at a conference in the diocesan retreat house, so was reasonably near. He was pleased to meet my friends, and seemed quite moved by the sight of me with the children in a real home setting – quite a different ambience from the rented cottage in Bletchingdon.

It was me this time who was suddenly affected by the bizarre nature of our relationship. Perhaps it was suddenly seeing him through Hilary's eyes; or maybe it was the simple fact of sitting at a table in the most pedestrian of pedestrian shopping precincts, outside the bookshop, having coffee with a black-habited Benedictine monk whom I hoped to marry in the near future! Yet our plans remained unchanged, and the uneasy feeling faded as we resumed our 'normal' correspondence.

In his next letter, David quoted from a book called *The Second Journey* by Gerald O'Collins, which seemed to have provided him with some sort of rationale for what he was going through. It was about 'mid-life crises', and he quoted some lines from the 'Afterword' by the psychiatrist Jack Dominian:

There is a small group of men and women who are described as loners, as isolated persons, who find it difficult to get close to others. They may cope with their isolation by remaining single, marrying someone who is equally impersonal, or entering religious life which does not demand personal closeness . . .

Gradually they find that their isolation is stifling, and become aware of an overwhelming desire to get close to somebody else . . . The religious life may be abandoned for a personal relationship of intimacy . . . There is a need to get close and share one's inner world with another and he or she becomes the first *significant other* in life, including – for the first time – God, who may be the channel through which trust is attempted and established (p. 90).

David explained in his letter that the passage quoted made him feel that he had some objective basis for what he was intending to do; that it wasn't mere 'selfishness', which he feared would be the public judgement upon him, but the build-up of irresistible inner forces which were recognized and documented by professionals. That I was the first 'significant other' in his life was made clear by his concluding words: 'I am astonished and filled with gratitude for the wonder and generosity of your love for me.'

He included in this letter a copy of the statute governing the resignation of the abbot with the key passages underlined:

Should the Abbot, by reason of ill-health *or any other cause* apart from those mentioned above, wish to resign his office, he shall place his resignation before the Chapter in writing, adding, *if he wishes*, the reasons which have led him to seek release from his office . . .

. . . Should fewer than two-thirds of the votes cast in secret ballot be in favour of accepting the resignation, the Abbot *shall be requested to continue in office, but it shall be within his competence, after consultation with the Visitor, to insist upon resigning by notifying the Chapter to this effect in writing*.

These formal words had a sobering effect, but also served to make the whole thing seem more real. A few days later – on 14 May – Sister Ben arrived with two of her novices for a visit to Nashdom Abbey. While the novices were being shown round, she and David had a chance to talk. She brought welcome news that there was a space available in one of the community's student houses in Oxford, if I wanted a place to stay between returning from Cheshire and going to Wales. She also told David that she thought Mother Frances should be told about 'us' fairly soon, in strict confidence, of course.

This was one of the contributory factors in a 'spiralling depression' that took hold of David after the visit. He tried to explain to me in his letter why he had found the idea so threat-

ening. It seemed to be a mixture of the nearness of the 'de-
nouement' and a fear of the exposure that could so easily
result if rumours once started to fly. He wrote as he was coming out of the depression, but it was revealing of his state of
mind underneath all the selfless avowals:

Sunday 16 May 1982

Yesterday I felt like a trapeze artist who, having let go of his
bar, can see no sign of the catcher. In that sense of deprivation, various despairing thoughts emerge. . . . Suffice it to
say that I wondered whether I had been so busy saying that
I love you that I had not given you space enough to ponder
whether you really love me, or opportunity to say if you do
not . . .

Part of the difficulty was, I think, the sense that our experience of loving has been so different. You have many dear
friends who can, for you, remain part of the rich texture of
your life, so that for you loving is by addition and multi-
plication. For me, loving you is the breaking of all the patterns, which I am pleased to do as loving you is the most
enriching experience of all my life, but it seems to be a
process of subtraction and division.

In the process of exploring his own arithmetical analogy, he
came to a definitive statement about his own experience of the
religious life, which has, I think, remained his truest statement
on the subject:

it has been characteristic of my life that most of its supposed achievements have been the result of saying 'no' to
people and things, and not of saying 'yes'. This is the fundamental weakness of my monastic life. Only in loving you
have I begun to say 'yes' to life, to people, and, ironically,
to God. My God had been a deified 'no'. I would never
want to say that monastic life prevents a true 'yes' to God,
but I do know that for me it never had been, and never
could be that.

Reading this I was profoundly conscious of the fact that the
fundamental weakness of my own religious and secular life
was the exact opposite – that of saying an indiscriminate 'yes'

to people and things, without counting the cost of fulfilling my commitment.

By the end of the letter he had pulled himself out of his depression, by dint of reading more Gerald O'Collins and seeing some hope for an honourable way out of his predicament.

For both of us, the sense of being in limbo was particularly hard to bear. Although I was still busy during my last weeks in Cheshire, and loved being with Hilary's sons, the sense of my own life being in abeyance was very strong. I wanted to get on with *doing* something, but was held back by my emotions, which were locked into David's struggle. Hilary and her husband were paying me the same amount of money as I had been getting on Social Security after the warehouse job had finished. It was more than enough for my needs, but I craved independence and a place of my own.

One of the greatest drawbacks of St Gregory's for me was the fact that you simply worked for your keep and the pleasure of being part of the community. If you were eligible for Social Security, most of it was to be paid into the joint funds. It all felt very temporary. Meanwhile, back at Nashdom Abbey, David was feeling the same sense of time dragging its feet:

> Time seems to be passing with agonizing slowness just now, but at least the positive thing is that the outcome is not in doubt, so it is only a matter of waiting. . . . If I can only get to my resignation without a 'show-down', that, I feel, is the main thing.

I told David of my qualms about St Gregory's, and he was apologetic that he had not sufficiently appreciated my difficulties while dwelling on his own. He agreed with me that I should at least go and visit them, and see how I felt when I was there.

We were both getting rather rattled by the waiting and the need for secrecy. He reiterated that he was dubious about my desire to tell Mother Frances about us, yet I was unhappy at the deception, which I was afraid would explode in our faces. Matters were not helped by the constant interruptions during David's phone calls, as monks burst into his office to demand all manner of things. It was almost as if they did it on purpose.

But time did pass; and I found it in me to be reasonably patient and generous. He was so fragile as the time approached that I knew I had to control my own frustrations in order to support him.

He had one or two close friends in the vicinity of Nashdom with whom he was able to talk frankly, and this helped him a lot. He wrote about a visit to one particular friend:

She recognizes and affirms the David Weston and attaches little significance to the Wilfrid I have fabricated, although she has come to know me in my Nashdom setting. If one sensible person can do that, perhaps there are a few others as well.

Yet on Monday, 24 May, there was a sudden new development. Brian O'Malley went to Nashdom to talk to David about St Gregory's becoming officially affiliated to Nashdom, and David told him our secret.

9

A Heart of Flesh

Understandably, Brian O'Malley was very upset at the effect that our plans would have on St Gregory's, as David was the key person in his negotiations with the abbey for oblate-house status. Being an ex-Roman Catholic Trappist monk, he was also appalled at an abbot contemplating such an action. He had in fact left his own community to marry, but had only been a junior monk at the time.

Nevertheless, Brian bravely undertook to tell one of the other 'guardians' of St Gregory's who lived nearby and was closely involved, in order to test his response. The four guardians at that stage were David, Sister Ben, the Bishop of Ramsbury and James Coutts, the Vicar of Brecon. It was the latter who Brian promised to contact. I had already met him briefly through Sister Ben.

In his letter on the following Sunday (30 May), David wrote that Brian had subsequently phoned, 'with some sense of urgency' to report James Coutts's reaction. Apparently, James had been 'most understanding and sympathetic', but also insistent that my existence remain a secret until after David had left. 'Father Coutts had obviously hoped that I might emerge with my reputation intact', David wrote in a rather forlorn tone, going on to say:

> The practical outcome of all this excitement is not only that Father James Coutts will be coming to see me, but it is likely that you may be urged directly or indirectly to be as secretive as possible. I say all that mainly that you should know that I am not 'behind it', trying to put any pressure on you.

He must have anticipated my reaction, which was to feel that the male ecclesiastical establishment was closing ranks to protect one of its number. I felt that I was again cast in the role of a 'dangerous woman', and was conscious not only of anger, but a sense of foreboding that they would do their best to squeeze me out. I feared I would be dispensable, having performed my function of revitalizing the abbot for the greater good of the monastic community.

Yet my cynical reaction was short-lived, because David's protestations that the 'world' (sic) was well lost for love disarmed me: 'Although it may be the instinct of James Coutts, and other fair-minded people, to "rescue" me, I am more than content – I am positively glad – to slip between their fingers and vanish out of their sight, if only it is to be with you . . .' The rest of this letter was full of his account of the Pope's visit to Canterbury, and his own memorable participation in the service at the cathedral.

It was a measure of the disparity of our lives at this time that David was in Canterbury Cathedral attending such a solemn religious occasion, while I was at a folk festival with my friends in Cheshire, camping out in an open field, and singing and dancing in the local pub, while clog dancers from Sheffield entertained us on the cobbled forecourt. This sense of the split-focus was heightened by my reading David's reverential account of the service (he was sitting 15 feet away from the Pope's chair at the foot of the high altar steps), at the same time as watching it on the news with my friends in Cheshire – who were deeply dismissive of the whole thing.

As I was preparing to leave Cheshire, David was preparing to go into hospital for a minor operation which had suddenly worked its way to the top of the waiting list. He was actually quite looking forward to it, as it would not only relieve him of some discomfort, but would give him time on his own to think and daydream.

One of his letters around this time gives a very vivid picture of his mood, showing him to be in a suspicious state of contentment. The monks must have found him a most tantalizing figure as he was 100 per cent efficient at controlling his facial expressions – but even he could not prevent the emanations of contentment that he knew were coming from him at this time:

At breakfast I was looking at Father James at the far end of the refectory and was wondering what he was thinking as he began his day. Some people I know are able quite easily to be content and happy. Looking back, for me, monastic days were to be got through, with the emphasis on achievement, or else the achievement of getting through the day and being ready for the next one. I suddenly realized how few days in my life I had been happy and that none of them had been here. And even my happiest of days had lacked 'the one thing needful' – to love and be loved.

At breakfast today I sat hoping that James had enough to live for today, myself feeling deeply content because of you – just that you are, and that my life, consequently had, for the first time, point, meaning, focus and direction.

He was working in the kitchen garden every afternoon, and for the week before the operation, both morning and afternoon. He was happiest gardening, I knew: 'Time slips away fast as I garden so it seems the best possible way of spending this week.' Nor was he indifferent to the fact that his skin tanned easily and that he was getting very fit with all the outdoor work.

In my last letter from Cheshire I told him in more detail about the folk festival, ending with the casual phrase, 'the three of us decided we would like to repeat it next year with you there. Would you come?' His reaction was guarded:

Those two simple sentences are so charged with weighty implications as to stand out from the rest of your letter, by reason of their simple practicality. They presuppose a world that I do not know and can barely imagine. A world in which I am with you; a world in which one is free to make choices . . .

While David was in hospital, I had moved into my new Oxford abode and set out my 'survival kit' of treasured pictures and books. It was something like my tenth move since leaving community. All the same, it was good to be back among friends and be in Oxford, though I was soon to be off on retreat again with Sister Ben. She was in good form, so we were both looking forward to spending some time in each other's company again.

In the event, the retreat was very relaxing – something I had somehow not expected. Ben and I had a lot of spare time, so there was a chance to walk and talk, and even to do some thinking. On our return, we managed to engineer things so that there was time for a few hours with David before we all went our separate ways. My mother and father found themselves hosts to two habited religious on one day (which they survived extremely well, with a little help from Sister Ben's charm and humour!). David, as ever, was a more complicated proposition for them, as they were still wary of his designs upon their daughter. For my part, I selfishly enjoyed having two of my favourite people in the house at once.

By the beginning of July, things were beginning to move again, for James Coutts phoned to arrange his visit to see David on the 6th. My own plans were also moving forward. On the weekend of 10/11 July, I drove across to St Gregory's to meet Brian and his wife Rosemary and their three children, and another member of the community, a PhD student nicknamed 'Mole'. They were all very welcoming, and my fears were quickly allayed. Apparently theirs were too, as we finalized our plans for my arrival later that month.

Sister Ben was also visiting with one of her novices, an American called Vicky, and the latter looked after me when I was gripped with a severe period pain on the morning of the next day. I was still feeling very wobbly in the aftermath of the pain when James Coutts arrived to 'have a talk to me'.

I remember Sister Ben's smile of reassurance as she passed me sitting in the chapel in the minutes before he arrived. I knew that James had been to see David only days before, but I didn't yet know the outcome of their discussions. I waited there full of dread that some awful sacrifice was about to be demanded from me.

In order to keep my mind off it all, I studied the chapel, which was my favourite room in the house. It had a sort of 'Tolstoyan' feel to it, with a wood-burning stove in the middle and a gallery all around it. It was at the heart of the house – both literally and figuratively – and was a frequent thoroughfare as you had to go through it to get from the shop to the kitchen. It was definitely not conducive to quiet contemplation, which was a relief just then. When James finally arrived, there was a rather awkward few minutes as everyone sat around and made polite conversation. He then suggested a walk so that the two of us could talk. Everybody else miraculously melted away.

It was a wild, stormy day, and there was something faintly comic about the two of us shouting our theological arguments into the teeth of the gale. At one point, James gallantly walked backwards so that we could catch each other's words more efficiently! When he finally reached the point of asking me to give David up, as I knew he would, the weather and the setting seemed satisfyingly wild and tragic, even to someone such as me – reared on *Wuthering Heights.*

I didn't yield without a struggle – in fact, I don't believe I promised anything. I countered his arguments about the sacredness of vows with my own sense that they had become dead letters to David, whereas my love had become a form of redemption to him.

James was an unusual priest – a rare combination of a compassionate, vulnerable human being with a ruthless lover of God. I was forced to see that God *might* be asking me to bow out, so that David could move on to greater heights in his vocation. He even made it seem like a privilege!

After this conversation with James, I felt very confused about my future at St Gregory's. Should I still be going there? Had things changed, or were our plans still fundamentally the same? The place was beautiful, the people congenial, but I had to see David. I didn't see him until the following Thursday, and waited nervously for his response, as I knew James was also going to write to him.

We had previously arranged that David would emerge from the monastery gates wearing his working clothes of jeans and shirt. I was to wait out of sight down the lane, and pick him up when he drew level with me. He had on his grey anorak with the hood up, and didn't turn his head until I drew level with him. The whole thing felt like something out of an old film. We drove through dappled woods in brilliant sunshine until we reached the Downs, where we could be comparatively free.

James's letter was in David's pocket. I could see he had opened it, but he passed it to me without a word, and waited for me to finish reading it before saying anything. Once I had absorbed it, I felt exactly as I had after my conversation with James. I couldn't see how anyone could resist the gentle ruthlessness of his logic.

It began by establishing that David had made a covenant love agreement with God through his vows – much as men and women do with each other in marriage – but that his experience of loving me had given him a 'new heart of flesh'. The old 'false Wilfrid' was breaking up like the alabaster box and he was being 'poured out'. Three things followed:

1. David must renew his gift of himself to God, in order to experience a relationship of depth and intimacy hitherto unknown to him.

2. He must apply what he had learnt about loving to the monks, and to see them no longer as a threat, but as individuals with hearts 'waiting to be remade into the beauty of ikons'.

3. He should not see me for at least six months – preferably a year.

The letter ended with this characteristic passage:

Either where you are, or with X, you will have to renew your offering of your heart to the Father: so it is better to do it now, in case you go to X and it is just on the 'level of need' and you regret it afterwards.

How very difficult. Particularly because X actually *delights* in God: is good: is true (and many other things). I think X's love is a true love – so true that X can see what I am asking of you and knows the options for you and the hurt it will cause X.

Don't let your chemistry (which has been bottled up for a long time) run away with you.

This interim period should not be filled with obsessions, but with the converted attempt to delight in God.

X knows of this letter and it might be good for X to see it for comments.

. . . From one unauthentic bloke to another, I pray for you both daily and whatever you choose, I am with you. This is how I see it at present, and I am trying to be open to the options and to the Good Father . . .

. . . I am scared of abbots and communities, but please phone or shall I come up?

If I had expected David's reaction to be just like mine, I couldn't have been more wrong. It was as if he had gone beyond such 'idealistic' solutions; as if the whole thing had gone on too long and that it was too late to make the enormous effort required to see everything in a new light. He seemed tired and old, but also quite resolute. I quote one or two key passages from the letter David sent to James in reply the next day:

First I want to say how deeply grateful I am to you for being at the same time so loving and so uncompromising. H and I find ourselves recognizing the authority of what you say, both in terms of its intrinsic validity, and in respect of the authority which we confer upon it by the seriousness with which we treat your words . . .

He then went on to say:

. . . to speak of my sense of brokenness you use the telling image of the alabaster box. It is not, however, an image that I can make my own. I myself see, perhaps, three phases of brokenness. The past phase, relating to the last ten years or so, has been one of my life haemorrhaging secretly and silently into the sand. The present phase is one in which I more readily admit to myself and to others my present weakness and need. The future phase will be the shattering of my reputation, which would be all to the good if others were not hurt and distressed by it.

Over against the experience of brokenness you set the love of God . . . Certainly the God of whom you speak is the God whom I am supposed to have served all my life. Yet in the daily experience of my monastic life it is another God whom I have served and borne witness to, for there is a real sense in which we make God in our own image. (Can it be that never having known a human father makes a difference here?) My God (sic) makes demands but does not give . . . In the early years it actually felt good to live by this understanding. More recently the sense of life soaking into the sand has removed its charm.

You speak, reasonably enough, as though, in loving H, and in beginning to dare to believe that she could love me, there had been effected in me that transformation whereby the heart of flesh replaced the heart of stone. Of course in a sense this is true, but the conclusion that I draw is different.

I encounter H not only as a loving and lovable person, but also as the only convincing sacrament of a love that is unconditional, making no demands. I can comprehend H as in some sense a gift and a revelation of the God of love. I can understand her as a temptation set before me by a God whose demands are total but gives nothing. I have more difficulty in understanding a God of love who shows me H as some sort of shock treatment.

Of course I know how I should view H from the monastic standpoint, but while loving H in order to give up loving her may be useful in impressing upon me the contractual nature of profession, it is not calculated to effect the transformation of the heart of which you speak.

The letter ended with David's promise not to 'manipulate events' and to wait upon the 'providentiality' of the outcome.

My strongest memory of that day is not the discussion we must have had over the letters, but of sitting in the car at the end of our time together, watching him walk away from me up the road to Nashdom with his athletic self-conscious gait. He didn't once turn round, and I was full of a sense of premonition, as I felt the barriers going up all around us.

Monday's letter contained a copy of the one he had sent to his sister-in-law's brother, Crispian, telling him of our plans. David had always had great affection for Crispian and had visited him often in his home in Devon. He was hoping that the two of us would be able to meet up when Poppy's family helped them move into temporary Oxford accommodation at the end of the month. Apparently, the archdeacon's lodging was not yet ready for occupation.

It would be my first meeting with Poppy and the 'children' (all in their teens), as well as her mother and brother, and I was apprehensive about it, wondering not only how they would react to me, but also how David would be in their presence. I knew that he had always felt in his brother's shadow, so it was painfully important that the meeting went well and that he felt affirmed.

It did not bode well that they had both expressed their reservations to David about the Welsh scheme. I think they felt that it wasn't a real solution, which was the way I was secretly beginning to view it myself. My own qualms were centred round its semi-monastic aspirations. It sounded like a sort of Welsh Little Gidding, with regular offices in the chapel punctuating their work on the smallholding and in the shop. Of course, there was nothing wrong with such aspirations in themselves; it was simply that they were wrong for me.

St Gregory's had even adopted a sort of monastic habit – inspired by Brian's experience as a Trappist monk in Scotland. It was a brown heavy-duty fisherman's smock, worn with a thick leather belt and corduroy trousers or jeans. For the offices they wore a sort of homespun hooded robe, which was simple and beautiful to look at, but very monastic in its inspiration.

The offices themselves were sensitively put together with a lot of informality and warmth, and live music played by Brian and Rosemary and any visitors who were so inclined. But all this did not prevent warning bells ringing in my head. I knew that I should not be playing this particular game anymore, but be out earning some money and independence for myself. However, things had gone too far, and too much was at stake. I was due to go to St Gregory's at the beginning of August.

Perhaps another of the factors in my reluctance to go was my own increasing sense of homelessness. Since the beginning of the year, I seemed to have been constantly on the move, and I was beginning to feel the inadequacy of living much longer on my survival kit. I was also relishing the proximity of Philippa, who had a room in the same house. By this time, she was already in a steady relationship with her future husband, Nigel, but she had been around through all my time in the convent and knew me at a depth that I was loath to forfeit at such a crucial stage in my life.

I had wanted David to meet Philippa – and Nigel – for a while, and I remember when we met up we all laughed a lot, particularly when David told his story about being pronounced 'clinically dead' by a doctor who was unable to elicit any knee-jerk responses from him with his hammer! I was relieved that Philippa liked David, and there was no denying that he cut an elegant figure in his black Benedictine habit.

That meeting with Philippa occurred the day after our grand encounter at Frank's and Poppy's house. David did a lot of gardening and I did a lot of talking, and it all seemed to go very well. Two of their grown-up children were there, as well as Poppy's mother, brother and an old friend, so my fears about meeting them all were over in one fell swoop! It was good to read in David's letter – two days later – that it had lived up to expectations for him too:

29 July 1982

> There was for me the important experience of feeling a wholeness and a completing by virtue of your presence such as I have never felt before. No longer do they represent joys in which I can never fully share. Now they are affirming what we can ourselves know, even more gloriously.

Soon after receiving this letter, I set off for Wales. My first days at St Gregory's were very mixed. In some ways they confirmed my worst fears, as I found it hard not to feel trapped, and even repelled, by the overtly religious lifestyle there. In addition, it was a shock for me to be in such deep country. It was so far away from anywhere and it was so dark, particularly at night when I stumbled down the field path to my primitive caravan.

Brian and Rosemary, who now preferred to be called by the Celtic names of Brendan and Morwenna, were both very friendly in different ways, though I found Morwenna's practical housekeeping and culinary talents daunting, and Brendan's religious views exasperating. Yet I could have coped with all that, and simply enjoyed the cut and thrust of it all and the wonderful food, if I had felt that I had something genuine to contribute; but there was nothing obvious.

On reading my early impressions of St Gregory's, David impressed upon me that I must not stay there for him: our plans could easily take another direction. He reiterated Frank's earlier offer that I could lodge in their house, as Poppy would not be living there till December, and Vicki, their middle child, was away at school.

However, things gradually settled down. I moved out of my caravan and into one of the bedrooms on the gallery. I got to know Mole, who became a good friend, and Jane, who had recently joined them, and I discovered some kind of ministry to the guests who came on retreat – to make up for my ineptitude in practical tasks! It was a time of waiting.

David was gradually telling the other communities he was involved with about his impending resignation, and their reactions were starting to come in. He wrote in his letter of 6 August:

6 August 1982

> Dom Gregory has just been to see me to say that the novitiate has now learnt that I am resigning from the Haggerston novitiate, who must have learnt it from my letter to their Mother, and any discussion she initiated as a result. The 'white water' below the weir will soon be in full view, so the line between us will soon be tested.

His engagements outside Nashdom were gradually dwindling, and he had no public engagements in his diary from October onwards. He was involved in a visitation of a Benedictine priory, and was impressed by the community's readiness to rally round as their young prior was being forced to resign through ill health. He didn't mention his own impending resignation, but felt the irony of the situation acutely.

There had also been another letter from James Coutts that was in the same vein as his last one, but David was disposed to believe that James had an idealistic view of community life, and preferred Mother Frances's letter, which affirmed his decision to leave and offered her support. He enclosed a photocopy for me to see.

She had written the first half of the letter in response to the talk that she and David had had in the presence of an American superior they both knew. In it she had assured David that they both felt it was neither right nor possible for him to remain at Nashdom, and that they both had no doubts of the integrity of his position. The second half of her letter was written after I had been to see her and told her about 'us':

> What can I say? My heart is so full for you both . . . I know it is going to be very, very hard and not many people will

understand, but if the delight of God and his love is at the heart of it, then it will not really matter. Surely the far greater scandal of the death of your spirit through remaining where you are would be the most tragic grief in God's sight . . .

Please promise me that if you should find it any help to talk at any time, you will tell me. I am not very wise, but I do care an awful lot . . . Helen knows I am suggesting this and approves!

Despite Mother Frances's very supportive and caring response, David's spirits soon plunged again when a friend who was also an oblate of Nashdom Abbey reacted in a passionately negative way to his decision. He had confided in her the full extent of our plans, so he was exceedingly vulnerable to her comments. He wrote to me concerning her letter:

It seemed a sample of what thousands of people will say and think. That my behaviour is disgraceful; it ought never to have been allowed to develop in this way; that it will be damaging and undermining for so many, and so on. She makes the particular point that to leave would be understandable, but to leave to marry would be unforgivable. There ought, therefore, for decency's sake, to be a gap of at least a year, so that no direct connection is made between the two.

As the time of David's resignation approached, I was accusing him – as usual – of idealizing me and not loving the real person. He was – as usual – turning it all inside and worrying about whether I would find him wanting when I 'really' knew what he was like. He was also finding it difficult to keep hold of his feelings, which were increasingly prone to 'ebbing and flowing', 'waxing and waning', and other such metaphors of flux.

He was also becoming more and more obsessed with the practical costs of living in the outside world, his own lack of capital, and the impossibility of 'dropping out' of the church establishment if he had to provide financial support for us. I kept telling him that I was equally capable of providing the financial support we needed, but as I was involved in unworldly schemes like St Gregory's at the time, I wasn't exactly a solid bet! When David analysed his most pressing anxieties, though, they came down to one central issue: what people would think of his actions. His deepest instincts were to take himself off to some remote corner of the country to avoid identification, but these plans were frustrated by the money issue. Hence his inner turmoil.

Within his community nobody was mentioning the resignation issue, but all the monks were on their best behaviour – 'rather like a dog which has devoured the Sunday joint and is now seeking some way of ingratiating itself!'

Meanwhile back at St Gregory's I had been seeking out a place for us to live after we were married. I had told Brendan and Morwenna the whole story, and they had generously entered into the romance of it all. Together we had worked out plans for making habitable a cottage on their land. It was basic, but in beautiful surroundings – rather like the 'summer house' at Varykino where Lara and Yuri hide out in *Dr Zhivago*. I sent David photographs and told him of the plan. It must have seemed a remote, impractical fantasy to him, but he responded in kind:

24 August 1982

> You are very much my 'Lara', but all too often the long-term prospect looks like the end of that book. At least they were united in his dying, so perhaps that is a happier ending than I have ever recognized; there is after all more than one death and one is for me imminent.

Pasternak's book was almost like a bible for David, as he had read it five times during his years in the monastery, and poured all his dreams into it. By comparing 'our' cottage to the one at Varykino, I had made a happy connection for him and he was able to turn from all his talk of nervous breakdowns and the fear of becoming a pariah in ecclesiastical circles.

On Monday, 30 August David attended his last public speaking engagement before coming to Wales. It took place at the annual National Pilgrimage in Walsingham, and he gave his 12-minute address at a big open-air Mass, which formed part of a procession through all the important sites of the village. There were 6,000–7,000 people present, three bishops, one of whom was the principal celebrant at the Mass, 60 concelebrating priests in chasubles, and as many again in albs and stoles. David processed with the other Guardians (of the shrine), dressed in a 'Guardian's mantle', and obviously felt satisfied with his last 'star appearance'.

Back at St Gregory's, I was able secretly to relive the glamour of the occasion through the eyes of a friend who had been present, and was describing her own painful emotional drama that had taken place in the context of the pilgrimage. Despite everything – and notwithstanding my friend's own personal pain – there was a deep pleasure in knowing that I was the most important person in David's life; it would have been dishonest to deny it. But for him there were also darker thoughts – of 'the ignominy of being struck off the list of Guardians' – as well as everything else.

However, he remained outwardly calm despite inner panics, and speculated whether his community was planning any form of counter-action. On the whole, he thought they were probably too divided among themselves to produce any form of concerted effort.

The key meeting would take place on 7 October, when the former abbot would be in the chair and David would be barred from the chamber. It was unlikely that he would ever know exactly what transpired on that occasion. At the September Chapter – on the 9th – he anticipated that they would only be dealing with 'the practicalities of the process'.

Now, at last, there was no public engagement coming between himself and St Gregory's. He was due to arrive on 12 September and stay for a week. Our future plans depended upon how he reacted to the place (and the cottage), and whether he could envisage fitting himself into the rhythm of life there. By this time, everybody at St Gregory's was getting into the spirit of the thing, and there seemed to be a suppressed air of excitement about the place. As the days were crossed off the calendar at David's end, life went on in its inexorable way at Nashdom, with community duties filling the time – cooking, gardening, feeding the wayfarers, attending recreation, etc. The post continued to arrive, including a very appreciative letter from Father David Hope, the then Vicar of

All Saints, Margaret Street, who was the new Master of Guardians at Walsingham:

31 August 1982

> This is just a brief note to thank you so much for your magnificent sermon yesterday at the National Pilgrimage. There was a great deal of approval and I know quite a large number of people to whom I talked were tremendously appreciative and enthusiastic.

It seemed profoundly ironic that the power of David's sermon had come from his own acute awareness of personal disintegration behind his monastic façade. The central symbol used in the sermon was the skeletal east window of the ruined Priory Church, which arched over them as they celebrated their Mass. David took it as a sign of the failure of man's ambition and his human frailty, but also as an indication of the resurrection that comes among us once we have accepted our brokenness. It seemed fitting to him that in this last official sermon he should be conscious of integrating his public reflections and his private discoveries. Yet it did leave him wondering, once again, where such gifts as he had could possibly be deployed once he had left.

There was now only a fortnight to go before David arrived in Wales, and he was spending his time reading the revised 'Declarations' (constitution) of St Gregory's in preparation for discussing them with Brendan during his visit. If they were acceptable, then affiliation of St Gregory's to Nashdom Abbey would go ahead. The blend of monasticism and family life contained in them seemed reassuring to David at that stage, though he knew that I found the combination problematic.

I had had a series of long talks with Brendan and Morwenna around this time, and we had come to the mutual conclusion that St Gregory's was not the place for me in any long-term sense. My rebellion against the 'robes' and the 'offices' and all the other trappings of monasticism was a clear indication to them that I needed to be out of community. It also seemed obvious to them that I was not a natural country girl – despite my protestations of love for the landscape – and needed the stimulation of a town.

I was quite shocked by their clear-sightedness, as I had believed myself capable of convincing anyone of anything if I tried hard enough! In the end, though, I was grateful for their straight talking as it took the struggle to conform off my shoulders, and allowed my real affection for them to flow unimpeded.

Thus it was decided for everything to go ahead as planned – if David agreed – and for the two of us to stay in the cottage for as long as we needed, but then move on to our ultimate destination.

10

Abraham and Isaac

I was dreaming a lot about David as the time for his arrival approached. The dreams were full of anxiety and urgency, and seemed to be building towards some sort of crisis. I quote from my journal, which I was keeping intermittently at the time:

Monday, 6 September 1982 – Journal Entry

I dreamt, two nights ago, that he was Peter O'Toole, as he had been in *Becket* – only here he was much older. He was in a great theatre, and he was walking down the aisle telling us all about his life and sufferings. He was an austere, deeply poignant figure, very thin, with suffering eyes. He was obviously seriously ill, and shouldn't have been there at all. Yet the audience was rapt by his story.

And I was too – hearing it as if for the first time – though also worried because he was so thin and ill. I knew all the way through that he was the abbot, and that he loved me – and the two facts were not in the least incompatible with this performance. I felt very ennobled by it – the love of such a tragic figure.

In the interval I went for a walk with him – we might even have gone home, I can't remember. I was in his arms, and he kissed me, and I was solicitous about his illness, advising him to go home, even though I longed for the anguished pleasure of seeing him perform again.

But he said, in a very rueful, boyish, weak way, 'He won't let me. He has given me a first-class return ticket.' It was peculiar; he was very much Peter O'Toole, and also the abbot, but he was speaking about the abbot as the stern, father figure who kept him in this weak, boyish thralldom.

The dream haunted me all day as I tried to understand what it meant; then in the evening he phoned. His voice sounded remote and impersonal as if he was describing something like a series of ecumenical dialogues. He told me he had come to the conclusion after conversations with a number of people, that he needed to be on his own to work things out for himself, and find out who he really was. There was much muttering about incompatibilities of character – and did we really know each other well enough?

My head said he was right – at least about the solitude – and he was only proposing what I had maintained all along, but I was filled with a kind of silent screaming: anger and panic and desolation all mixed up together. When I told him my reaction, he didn't retract anything. There was no springiness in his voice, only deadness. He said he would phone back later.

Although I continued to feel desolate and frightened, I knew as the evening progressed that I had to do the generous thing and give him the space he needed, without pressure or drama. So I wrote him a letter in which I said that I agreed with his decision to do the inner work on his own, and that I would wait for him. I told him he needn't feel pressured or anxious about me, that I would go back to Oxford and get a proper job, so that when we did come together it would be the free choice of two 'whole' people. It felt as if I wrote the letter in blood. I didn't want to be out in the wilderness pretending to be busy and fulfilled while he suffered. I wanted to be indispensable to him, as I had always been.

But something in me was also aware that it wasn't dignified and it wasn't safe to be that exposed. I had been too reliant on our joint future. It was necessary to retract, consolidate, before the branch I was sitting on was sawn off. I knew I must not invest my whole self-esteem, my sense of meaning, in one human being. Ever again. Not after the convent.

The image in my head as I wrote the letter was that I had to allow myself to fall away from him in the dark – like a booster rocket which is used up in propelling the main rocket into outer space, but how could I bear to be that selfless?

In response to my letter, David replied as follows on 7 September 1982:

It is . . . wonderful to me that you should be so understanding and patient with me, really to accept me as I am when I am so little disposed to accept myself. I do realize this is at great cost to yourself, and in no sense do I minimize this. Nothing so substantiates my own feeling of rightness about it all as your readiness to wait upon, rather than force, the outcome.

Please do not think that I feel nothing for you, that is very far from the case. I love you very much, but I see you at the moment like a tree rising from the centre of a maze; in view, but with myself still separated from you by many twists and turns.

He ended his letter with the assurance that he was: 'flooded with a new hope and a new confidence in the rightness of it all, and with love and gratitude and joy'.

The sense of gratitude and peace was such that he even found himself looking forward to the Chapter which was due to take place two days later.

I never heard the outcome of that Chapter. I presume the monks debated the form which the resignation chapter meeting should take, deciding on all the necessary procedures and rituals. I expect it passed without incident because David was always a master of protocol and the management of committees.

From this point on events began to escalate.

20 September 1982 – Journal Entry

I must try and set down everything that happened after I wrote the letter saying I would wait for him.

After I had done it, and while I was waiting for the reply, there was an almost physical sensation of heaviness and deadness in me. It lasted from Monday until I got his letter on Thursday or Friday. I identified the sensation quite precisely one day; it was the absence of a quickening of love inside me, as if the 'baby' I had been carrying inside me had actually gone dead.

When I got his letter this feeling went, as it was full of joy and liberation. The answering joy I felt was both pure and intoxicating – like breathing 100% oxygen. After that, right up until he came, all I felt was intense excitement and anticipation, coupled with the conviction (shared by Morwenna and Brendan) that David's healing could take place at St Gregory's, but that my place was back in Oxford with a career and independence – until he was ready.

But then he actually came – and there was something wrong from the start. Well, not exactly the start – as the look on his face, as I crossed the chapel to be taken in his arms, had the same famished intensity as ever (despite the embarrassment of my being in the middle of serving in the shop and Brendan being there on the sidelines).

But, after that, things went increasingly downhill. I don't know quite what it was. Partly, my reaction to him was jagged: compared to Brendan's warmth and spontaneity, he was stiff, gauche, formal. And he seemed to miss all the opportunities to smile, touch, or even relate to me. I somehow felt disconnected from him – as if he hardly knew me. In choir he seemed so terribly austere, his features so impassive. He seemed to choose the monk's role rather than the human role so often. It felt as if our relationship was deteriorating fast – and even when we were alone for brief spaces, I just felt deeply uncomfortable and confused. The intimacy was just not there.

When I engineered his walking me to the gate after Compline, and he kissed me in the same perfunctory way, I said something like 'Well, I hope tomorrow is better than today has been.' I was sure that he would take me up on this and discuss with me what had caused the awful jangling between us; but he didn't, and quite brusquely dismissed me, saying we'd talk in the morning. I felt rejected and humiliated, and wondered if I had caused his withdrawal by unconsciously siding with Brendan's warmth, earthiness and humour against David's austerity. (Brendan had incidentally said that night, I think – or maybe at Matins – 'That man is 100% a monk, and you will have to see that' – or words to that effect).

The next morning was just as strained – but partly relieved by the fact that we were all out 'lifting' potatoes. I continued to feel disconnected from him, wondering all the time at his ease in answering monastic questions from the other guests, and moving in the theological framework, when I thought him so alienated from it all.

But then the answer came. That afternoon we went for a walk up the hill known locally as Crystal Mountain, and he told me his 'decision' – in the kind of tone a doctor uses to tell you you have terminal cancer. We walked up the steep track in single file without touching. It was very hot; we hardly spoke. I kept thinking I had to repair this awful breach by taking his hand or saying something, but I was paralysed, and also humiliated, so that my pride kept telling me that he should make the first move.

When we at last sat down at the top, with our feet dangling over the edge, looking out over that wonderful view which Morwenna always described as the 'kingdoms of the world' I was filled with a kind of premonitory dread. I hardly know how to describe what it was that he finally blurted out. I had to drag it out of him, stage by stage, and even as I was doing it I didn't realize the import of what he was saying. I even wondered by his embarrassment, if he was going to tell me he was homosexual.

He seemed embarrassed about some sort of 'image' that had surfaced powerfully from his unconscious and had refused to go away; it was clear that he regarded it as authoritative. He said that in the 'image' he was pregnant, and I was the father of 'the child'. He seemed embarrassed that he could have experienced himself as female, and even more embarrassed that he could have imagined himself pregnant. Yet he didn't seem in any doubt that the image was his own personal brand of revelation, with all the authority that that carried. He added that he was afraid that I wouldn't want 'the child'.

His grave, portentous manner was beginning to get to me by this time and I became tense and bad-tempered, demanding him to tell me who or what this 'child' was, and what did he mean by saying that I didn't want it. When he confessed that 'the child' was the new birth of his monastic vocation I was somehow completely unprepared for it, and the enormity of what he had said hit me with its total force before I could protect myself. I felt winded, as if I had been physically punched in the solar plexus. I can't remember what I did – except I think I sat with my back to him in silence for several long minutes, gasping for breath, trying to take it all in when my whole physical being was expelling it in horror and revulsion. Inwardly, I was talking not to David, but to God, shrieking 'No! This is too much. You *can't* ask this of me. No, no, no!'

I was flooded with thoughts of Abraham and Isaac and the demand to sacrifice everything I held most dear – as a *test*.

Everything fell away, and I was alone. I doubted God fundamentally. I don't know how much of this came out verbally or in what order. I know that there were sobs and shouts at David – so he certainly knew my terror and desolation, my shock, disbelief, anger, bitterness. But always the awful knowledge that it was final – something in his manner had subliminally told me that. And the way he comforted me was from a position of strength and calm and resolve. Even when he told me that the decision lay with me – to accept or kill 'the child' – I knew it was a hollow option, and told him so in no uncertain terms.

He was asking me to affirm the new life in him, the integration, the integrity of his response, despite his personal wishes. I *knew* I had to, knew it was the only way through, and yet I had to do it in the midst of this tearing, negative reaction of bitterness and loss. I felt I would be destroyed by the conflicting impulses. And the terrible sense of rejection: of me, the particular, personal me, with a body and a future and day-to-day needs. He kept assuring me that he loved me, and that all this was only possible because of my love for him, but I felt as if his behaviour denied his words. Because somewhere he was invulnerable – he didn't cry or shout or break down in any way. There was just this gentle, understanding acceptance of all that I could hurl at him. It was more terrible and final than any threats or anger could have been.

Even when I finally crossed the terrible physical space between us and threw myself into his arms in convulsive sobs, saying that I just wanted him and that nobody else in the world could comfort me, even then, though he said how much it had hurt him too, I felt it changed nothing. Through the following hours and days he inexorably receded from me, until I actually felt I had to ask him if I was boring him with all this weeping and talk of never-agains. He was always unfailingly courteous and kind, but became less and less the David I had known, and more and more the monk.

Yet that first day there was still great comfort in his touch and his tenderness when I came back to find him in the evening. He had been looking for me, and his mere offer of a gin and tonic started me weeping again. We sat out on the terrace overlooking the mountain sunset. It was like a hundred other similar encounters. All that evening and the next day in Tregarron, a nearby village, I still felt a great sense of ease and pleasure in holding his hand and walking close to him in the old way. At times it seemed too familiar for all the horror to be true. At other times the ease of our conversation – his ease in particular – seemed almost macabre. Often the whole thing seemed like a sick joke.

When we went to see James Coutts, I almost greeted him with the bitter comment that he had got what he wanted. Instead, I said something banal like 'the sky has fallen in', and started to cry. As soon as he had grasped what we were saying, he was so kind and loving that I could not be angry or bitter with him. In fact I warmed much more to him humanly speaking than to David.

When he admitted that, yes, he had got what he wanted, and there was a sense of joy and affirmation of his faith in God, he also seemed genuinely upset, and near to tears. He said that he had since got to know us as individuals and seen the human cost. And when I was crying, he took my hands in his, and was so deeply sympathetic that I cried even more.

The more David tried to explain his change of heart, the more he tried to justify his position, the more it seemed to me that he condemned himself out of his own mouth. He professed concern for me, but he seemed so absorbed in his own revelation and the contemplation of his future actions, that he kept bringing the conversation back to that, even when James had actually asked about me.

I kept having an uncomfortable feeling that *James* cared more for me as an individual woman and human being than David did. For David, I was like some counter he was moving about, some kind of figure in an inner drama of his own. And, once more, I saw – and hated – the terrible self-absorption of the religious life. I knew then that my place was on the side of ordinary life, of jobs and marriage and children, all the ordinary, messy, humanizing things. Even as David was talking about brokenness and suffering, and the way his ministry would be radically different in the future, I thought this is even now becoming cerebral, metamorphosing into the material for a good sermon.

Then when David began his 'voracious gardening', doing some weeding for James, and talked humorously about how he only really enjoyed uprooting, clea.ing and destroying, I knew that he meant it; and I felt 'This man is *alien* to me – the negative traits in his personality have been exalted as heroic asceticism, but the whole thing is deeply ambivalent.' I wasn't sure then if I really believed in this new heart stuff.

There was a lot more talk, but I knew nothing was going to change. My grief felt as if it were becoming rather grubby. So I left on the Friday afternoon, after David had helped me pack up, considerate as ever. It was the day before my thirty-third birthday, just three days after David had arrived at St Gregory's.

11
Coming to Terms with Grief

I drove home to my parents' house in Berkshire. Fleur sat beside me on the passenger seat for the long journey back. Not surprisingly, my birthday was a mournful affair – dispatched as soon as possible.

On the 21st there was a letter, and my heart leapt. Perhaps he had changed his mind? But no, it was a valedictory letter, celebrating a past love:

> You were so wonderfully understanding and valiant for the 24 hours before you left, but I know that it would be too much to hope that this has continued. I know that you must feel, at least to some extent, rejected and unloved, and that protestations from me to the contrary will seem invalid.

I wrote the following in my journal:

Tuesday, 21 September 1982 – Journal Entry

> I wish I had written in this book some account of the joy and the love and the mysterious hope that grew slowly. Now it is hard to remember what it felt like to be in that quickened state. I feel nothing most of the time – as if nothing had happened.
>
> I don't feel paralysed, its more like restlessness – urgent but aimless. I keep wanting to buy things – a duvet cover, a skirt. Habitat was very bright and reassuring today – perhaps the association with success. Also the prospect of a last-minute trip to Spain with Mum and Dad (they go in ten days and there's a cancellation) seems terribly important. And coffee. And Fleur. The usual components of comfort, I suppose.
>
> At some deep level I feel too exhausted and too numb to do anything but will to remain where I asked to be – at the centre of whatever fire God is thrusting me through. I don't want to evade or go off at a tangent. I want to go through the heart of the truth of it all even if it burns.
>
> But all that seems melodramatic as well. I veer between anaesthetizing myself with Radio 1 full volume and

obsessively reading books that deal with terrible things, like *Peter Abelard* and *Till We Have Faces* and Yeats's last poems.

Ever since Crystal Mountain he has signed himself 'David–Wilfrid', as a sign, I suppose, of the new integrated figure he believes himself to be. His letter-writing style has reverted to the pattern of the beginning of our relationship – theological, fatherly, and full of an impersonal gratitude. It is driving me mad.

David's final letter before my departure for Spain on 30 September conveys the flavour of his communications at this time very well. And although I know it gave me no comfort at all at the time, I can see now that there was a simple honesty about it, even a kind of dignity:

26 September 1982

It is strange not having a future, but only a past; but I would not have it otherwise were it not for your pain and distress, which I pray may yet find its fruition. Where I am seems to be where I have been put. It may not be pleasurable, but at least it ought to be possible.

This is not the letter that I would have wished to have written, but at least it comes to you without artifice. It comes with my love and gratitude, hoping for your sake and not mine, that you may yet see something of value emerge from it all.

Please do not doubt that I did love you and do love you with such love as I am capable of. That seems to be woven now into the structure of my life, which has needed it so much. You are more loved and more lovable, so you did not have the same need.

I hope you will enjoy Spain and soon find a congenial job . . .

With my love and prayers

David

At least we were back to 'David', even if temporarily. I wrote in response:

29 September 1982

Dear David,

If I can possibly keep myself to it, this will be the last time
I write to you for a while, partly because of the danger of an
explicit letter arriving in your absence, and partly because I
cannot bear the dissonance of your writing and feeling on
one level, and my doing so on another, which don't connect
at all.

I absolutely understand all the noble spiritual stuff you
say, and I accept it intellectually, as I would a book of au-
thentically written spirituality. I even feel a kind of poignancy and pride in your description of the way your love has
become woven into the texture of your life. That is how it
should be – and should always have been – and I rejoice for
you, even with you . . .

You are quite right: it is the fulfilment of all we spoke of in
those early days – the concrete and the soil, all that lovely
imagery. It was always about the feminine – and now you have
internalised it all and that is bound to be deeply beneficial for
you. I know too that it will hurt, because growing does.

But my experience of your shock revelation is not primarily spiritual; it is uncarnational – if you want to use
theological jargon. And I am left weeping and shouting in a
degrading fashion for *things* which we were supposed to be
sharing together, and which you do not seem to be lament-
ing the loss of *at all*.

Did we not plan a *home, children*, a specific place and manner of life? Did we not share physical intimacy and talk of
the time when we could explore the full implications and
release of physical union? Did we not get to know each
other's personality traits and physical mannerisms and
needs *in detail*? Or did I imagine it? All these things have
ceased to exist – *suddenly* – as if somebody had brought
down a whacking great macheté with terrible force . . .

How can you expect me to look at it from the neat structured familiarity of the religious life where everything has
meaning and continuity, by the very rationale of the life?
How *can* I look at it in the measured way you do?

OK, I don't want to soil or spoil the lovely thing that has transformed your life. I am *glad* I have had a hand in it. But now I must just keep my distance from you while the ugly, degrading reactions work themselves out. Because even though I hate you a lot of the time, I still love you and care for your honour . . .

But, if you can do it for me – sometime – please write down for me an account of our love – leaving *nothing* out. Saying what it meant to you.

What was the whole relationship for? Were you always *really* a monk who just needed an experience of love/the feminine? Or was our relationship a valid option, that nearly came off, but not quite?

Answer me, please, if you can. I am tormented by these questions.

Love Helen

I caught the plane to Spain with my parents on 30 September 1982, and I wrote in my journal a week or so afterwards:

10 October 1982 – Journal Entry

It was during the early morning car journey to Gatwick that the numbness began to wear off and I started to *feel*. I was huddled up in a corner of the back seat. It was still not light outside; I felt like a little girl again, a daughter. All I could feel was loss.

For the first half of the week in Spain it was the same kind of process as those first hours when he told me – as more and more situations came up in which I had to register the *loss* of him, the death of a future together: sunbathing, swimming, eating out, walking in the sun – all the things we might have done together as a married couple, particularly on a honeymoon. My parents were incredibly sympathetic and sensitive, but I didn't want them, only him. That made me feel bad too – and the way I was a dampener on their holiday.

In the days and hours after the holiday, my frustration grew to a pitch where I felt I had to express it face to face. I had to know what he thought it all meant. Why was I the *father* of his child/vocation? I felt used. I was obsessed by the fact that I had to make him express his own pain and loss, or somehow the whole thing was vitiated for me. It was as if I had dreamt it all, wasted two years, when I should have been getting on with my own life – and all for nothing. Did God really prefer males – and powerful important males – just like his church? I tried to get in touch with David. This was not an easy task at any time, but it turned out that he was away in Walsingham, at a Guardians' Meeting.

Then a letter from him arrived, written on Monday, 10 October. He had offered his resignation the previous Thursday at the Chapter meeting, but it had not been accepted. The community hoped that he would continue to lead them 'in the way of God'.

He wrote:

Meanwhile Westons and Athorpes alike show themselves less than enthusiastic at how things have worked out. In addition various influential Catholic-minded lay people have learnt that 'the Abbot of Nashdom is leaving to marry a nun'. Naturally I hope this rumour may diminish rather than grow, but, of course, I have only myself to blame, and obviously the news was too exciting for it to have been reasonable to hope that it would not be spread about. I try not to wonder who it was.

In his last paragraph, after expressing his penitence for the sorrow he had caused me by not 'perceiving the strength of the underlying commitment' of his vocation, he left it to me to decide whether we should communicate with each other again or not. In response, I wrote to book an appointment with him in the 'parlour' at Nashdom Abbey, and received in return a note giving three possible dates. I chose 29 October, from 10.15–2 p.m. (lunch and afternoon cup of tea provided). He seemed to be very conscious of sending his letters off to an uncertain reception, and hoped that face to face we would be more sure of understanding each other – though he was also conscious that he would be under some constraint in his monastic persona.

October 29 was a Friday. I was ushered into a dreary room at Nashdom Abbey, with high windows and flaking paint. In my memory, the picture is something like an interrogation room in a prison. David assures me there were no rooms like that, so I must have reconstructed it to fit my mood. He, on the other hand, has no memory of the interview at all, though it lasted five hours.

I wrote it down in my journal, to try to exorcize it, so perhaps that gives it undue permanence for me, but the experience remains like a blister in my memory, which I cannot touch without pain.

Friday 29 October 1982 – Journal Entry

I want to try and say what happened when I went to see him yesterday. Arrived at 10.35 and left at 4.15. We talked in one of their awful waiting-rooms or parlours, with red leather chairs and dirty window-sills and cracked plaster. There was a prie dieu with the confessional stuff on it, and a picture of the head of Christ carved at La Trappe.

David brought me some hideous warmed-up coffee on arrival, and some quite reasonable tea in the afternoon.

He started by saying that he agreed it was right he should be in his habit, and the meeting should take place at Nashdom, but he wanted me to bear in mind how difficult he found it to talk in personal terms in that setting and dress. He could not be natural.

It was a well-judged comment because the experience was like talking to pure intellect – my words and my pain bouncing off marble. He was so far withdrawn from me that it really was more or less impossible to tell if he felt anything *at all* for me.

The more I tried to elicit a response from him, the more he veered away from me, almost blatantly taking refuge in intellectualisms and tangential subjects. But towards the end of the morning he got a bit mad and said there was no point in my talking in one language and he in another when there was no point of contact. I said – in despair – that as far as I could see I was only talking in the language of loving: could he not respond at all in that language?

He said that our ways of responding were very different; it didn't mean that he didn't care. It was just that my way was to respond immediately and fiercely, whereas his response had kind of gone underground, and he would feel it in the years to come.

There was a sense of a massive weight of feeling dammed up inside him, never to come out. Part of the effect of this was the impression of someone who could not relate, who could talk of love but not communicate it, so that there was no bridge. It was as if the circuit was completed inside himself, and so was cold, egotistic and sterile. But there was also the painfully poignant image of the little boy who *longed* to love and be loved, with all the depth and passion of a very responsive heart – and who had had to hide it so long that it was now impossible to hope for anything else.

I tried to get him to express his feelings of loss but he didn't seem to feel he had any right to such feelings. He talked about the dangers of self-pity and the need to get on with the job. I protested that if he didn't take the risk of acknowledging his feelings, then the whole thing had been in vain. He would not be enriched or humanised by it all; on the contrary he was in danger of doing exactly the same blanket job on his feelings for me as he had over his commitment to the monastic life during our relationship.

That hurt him, almost exasperated him, and he said he wasn't that kind of person – he couldn't do it my way. There wasn't going to be any short-term dramatic humanisation in him. It would be long and slow.

What had really been shattered, he felt, was his pride and his self-respect. He felt he had betrayed me, betrayed the religious life, betrayed the close friends and family who had known about us; and now all he could do was endure it, live with that, and let it percolate through him. He seemed to feel that the simplicity of the monastic life – and particularly the lack of outside engagements that he had engineered for himself – would somehow give him a kind of integrity, if he just tried to live it wholeheartedly.

There was a kind of brokenness in him as he talked about his new way of living from moment to moment – like someone who has been involved in scenes of great carnage and become very simple as a result – almost with the radiance of a child. This was a truer reaction, I felt, than all his attempts at intellectual answers – or at least it was, in my terms. It reminded me of how I felt in my half-way house: sitting in the ruins, and building with the brick-dust. No further to fall.

He said that I had been a unique experience in his life – the only time he had loved and been loved. He insisted that he had not deserted me, I must not use that image. I should think of him as someone who had died. He told me that he loved me no less, thought about me no less. In fact, the knowledge of having been loved was a source of energy and meaning that he felt he would draw on all his life.

There was something unbearably sad about that, and I felt that somehow I must be able to gather up in my arms all the pain and anger and bitterness and loneliness I felt and dump it somewhere where it could not hurt him.

I knew that that was the only gift I had left to offer him. He had made his choice whatever the inner work or reactions which would follow in the long term. 'Here I stand; I can do no other' seemed peculiarly apt in his case. The sense of powerlessness and pain before that stance was total and fierce.

I had to take it and me out of the environs of the abbey before I gave way to the desire to set fire to the place, or to fall upon him in a fury of emotional blackmail and tears. It suddenly made me realize how Mum and Dad must have felt when they drove away from the convent and left me there.

I bought a new record so that I could drown my thoughts when I got back to the flat. Never had the future seemed so empty.

12

Divergent Paths

The following year saw our love story trailing off into a stagnant backwater. For me, it was a year of coming to terms with grief, and trying to stave off inertia and meaninglessness. I was often angry and often in tears, and I wasn't particularly successful in building an independent life for myself, though I wanted to do so, with a ferocity that had no real stamina or direction to it.

Looking back, it was a bleak and arid year, but something must have been achieved in the months from October to August 1983 because I got to the end of it with a responsible job to go to and three-quarters of my book on the religious life finished. Yet the reality was that I relied heavily on friends and family. Rosemary offered me a place in her flat again, and then after two months I was able to move into the flat above her which had become vacant. It seemed an ideal arrangement until the house that Rosemary had been hoping to buy also came on the market and she moved out – to a village near Woodstock. By the time winter came, there was a new tenant down below and I had to rely much more on my own company.

Wendy took me out to lunch regularly once a week, talking to me as if I were a normal human being with opinions and interests, rather than someone who was barely surviving, and other friends made sure I had some kind of social life.

From October to March I existed on Social Security while I applied for a variety of jobs without much conviction. I structured my time by working for a set number of hours each day on the book. But it was hard going, as the subject was too near the bone for any sort of critical distance, and kept dragging me back emotionally.

My family tried to help, but I was afraid of succumbing completely if I once let go, so I remained subbornly independent. In March 1983 I persuaded Oxfam to give me a job in their Mail Opening Department, for which I was grossly overqualified – but then, so was everybody else, with doctors of philosophy as well as ordinary graduates fighting to open the donations from the public. As before, the routine helped to humanize and stabilize me, but random communications from David could overwhelm three months' progress in an instant, which angered those closest to me – particularly Rosemary.

He rarely wrote, and phoned even more infrequently, but there are one or two letters from this year, two face-to-face meetings, and many encounters in my dreams. Both the letters and the two chance meetings were in 'abbatial mode', and did nothing to alter the impressions left by our last meeting in the parlour at Nashdom: he was living a life of quiet integrity within the community, and had successfully 'internalized' me so that he could draw strength from me without having to see me in the flesh.

My dream encounters were clearly an attempt to come to terms with this changed state of reality. There was a recurrent dream in which we were always out walking in the same country lane, happy and relaxed together, until we came to a stile. At that point in the dream, a bell would sound, the call-bell for Mass or the monastic office, and a stream of monks would flow purposefully by. David would join on the end without a word, or even a backward glance.

As summer approached, I was beginning – cautiously – to emerge into the light. My upstairs flat was in a leafy part of north Oxford, and the sunshine enticed me out on my newly acquired secondhand bike that I had sprayed bright blue. I went to the occasional concert and film, and even became involved in an outside broadcast for a BBC Religious Affairs programme. It was beamed out from my tiny flat on 24 July, with two huge pantechnicans and their monstrous aerials blocking the road most dramatically.

Rosemary and my sister Liffy both took part in the programme, and it did much to boost my self-confidence. In fact, it was a measure of my new-found independence that David rang to wish me luck on the day (I had written him a card to tell him it was on) and I hardly reacted at all.

One of the factors in my improved social life was suddenly meeting up with my ex-boss from Oxfam days. I think initially he was fascinated with my convent experience, because he had recently had a type of religious conversion himself, but he went out of his way to befriend me and take me out for meals.

Later, things became more complicated as he wanted more of a romantic involvement, and I was shocked to discover how much I still felt bound to David – though I knew there was no future for us. Our relationship went through several hiccups as a result of this, but levelled out sufficiently for him to feel able to offer me a job running one of his new bookshops at the Liverpool Polytechnic, starting in the autumn term. It was too good an opportunity to miss – at last there was something worthwhile to work for. So I prepared to move, and to leave behind all the painful memories of Oxford.

Then David got in touch again, and wrote to suggest we meet up while he was in Oxford house-sitting for his brother at the beginning of August. We were alone together in the house, and amid recriminations and anger there were a few brief moments of physical tenderness and desire. Yet for me it was a predominately bleak experience, and didn't alter my decision to pack up and head north. David, on the other hand, went away on his 'rest' with various relations and friends of the family, fired by the renewed contact between us and missing me 'colossally'.

He also reported that his monastic life was 'coming apart at the seams', leaving a trail of 'sawdust'. Discussions with Frank and Poppy (and his cousin Brenda) while he was on holiday encouraged David to believe that it was imperative he take several months' leave of absence from the monastery to sort himself out. On his return, there was a routine Chapter meeting about the garage conversion, during which the monks suddenly attacked him for his 'lack of leadership'. He described it in a letter to the Bishop Visitor as a 'fully justified indictment of my abbacy'. In fact, he felt massive relief that the monks had made the first move, and confessed to them spontaneously that he had long felt inadequate to the task and believed it was time for a new sort of leadership – one that was much more shared.

David's excitement at what had occurred pushed him into writing to me a few days after the meeting – on 31 August – although he had by then no idea where I was. The letter was forwarded by my mother to my brother's house in Southport, where I was staying until my parents retired and moved to Southport themselves, at the beginning of October.

The job at the bookshop was due to start in mid-September 1983, and the plan was that I would eventually find a place of my own in Southport and continue to commute into Liverpool each day – only 40 minutes by train.

David's next letter told me that he was now quite determined to resign, at the next scheduled Chapter Meeting on September 13. He addressed me as 'My Darling Helen' and promised 'I will not let you down a second time'. He concluded with the comment, 'I am sure it will have been worth the extra year's wait'. It had not felt like 'waiting' to me. Perhaps I replied rather too precipitately:

Dear David . . .

I am not the person I was a year ago, ready to follow you anywhere and adapt myself indefinitely. I have had to become independent; I have had to build my own life and the fault is *yours*.

Unlike you – to judge from today's letter – this last year has not been one of *waiting* for me. It has been an arduous, painful struggle to get over your rejection of me and learn to see a value in myself, independent of your love. With this job at the bookshop I have finally managed it – I have found some kind of status and responsibility and challenge which gives me back my self respect, and a measure of financial stability.

It's only in the last few weeks that you have given me any indication that you had not completely forgotten my existence. I can only assume you had no idea of the boredom, embarrassment, indifference, coldness, etc. that your voice has conveyed to me this last year – over the phone, in letters and even in person . . .

What I am trying to say is that because of the lack of hope on my side there came a point in this last year when I turned my back on you: it was like some kind of snapping inside. I became angry at my dependence on your love and the abject state it had reduced me to – and I resolved from then on to make my *own* way . . .

If you really want me, and really love me, you have to fight for me. Perhaps – to put it another way – there is some old-fashioned wooing to do. As I feel now, I would be

frightened to marry you, with so much unresolved between us . . .

I should think it needs to be said by now that I *am* thrilled
by your decision. I *am* impressed by this totally new determination, and I look forward with extreme longing to the
news that you are 'out' and beginning to live a *real* life again.

I *long* for a relationship in which we can both let go and
unravel the things which are so deep within us that we have
never dared let them out before. But it will not be easy.

With much love,

H

David didn't receive this letter until the evening of 6 September 1983. In ignorance of its contents, he went ahead
with his preparations to resign. On Saturday, 3 September,
he preached in Westminster Cathedral, an occasion that he
regarded as a 'temptation in the wilderness' – in other
words, to stay on as abbot for the kudos of such occasions.
Then on Monday, 5 September, he read a brief statement to
the Chapter at Nashdom, putting the case for his resignation
in favour of a shared style of leadership. It was not a formal
offer of resignation and there was no discussion of the pro-
posal. That was reserved for the meeting on 13 September.
But it went well, and he felt everything was going according
to plan.

On Tuesday, the 6th, he set off for Oxford as planned, to
meet with his brother Frank and Mother Frances. They had a
long and wide-ranging discussion about the options open to
him, and their joint conclusion was that he should resign
quickly and then go away for a period of at least six months.
All this support gave him a great sense of relief. On his return,
though, he found my letter waiting for him; the following is an
extract from his response:

Tuesday, 6 September 1983

Your letter has had the most profound effect on me. With
love I would say that I find it strangely distorted . . . It was
you who both introduced the idea of marriage and pressed
the pace towards that end, both by word and by practical

126

development, such as meeting your family. Because I loved you I went along with this, even though it posed problems for me . . .

I do not fully accept that I 'rejected' you last year, although I can understand that you put that interpretation upon it. In fact, having tried to keep up with the pace you had set me for ending my monastic life, eventually the whole thing backfired on me as so many minor problems were simply being ignored. I know it looked like rejection, but it was not the heartless and cynical decision that that word implies.

If since last year I have seemed to neglect or forget you, that was an amalgam of shame, uncertainty, a sense of uselessness, and a dozen other involuntary responses. I have always loved you, and although that love may have been offered in an unsatisfactory and useless way, it was always there.

Your anger at your dependence on my love was, I believe, a necessary step for you. You do not like to be dependent, as you many times made clear, and although it is not perhaps natural to me, I did not mind depending on you because loving you I was pleased at least to try to be what you wanted.

. . . Your letter shows that you have worked me out of your system. For you, there is a clear way ahead, and healing will be rapid if not already complete. So also for me. Although my day with Frances brought us absolutely to the conclusion that I must resign as abbot, your letter changed that as absolutely. I realized that I could continue here, healed by your love (even if now withdrawn) and healed by my love for you, which in its useless way will continue. I realize I do love my brethren, and realizing that, I realize I do love God – as from yesterday! . . . I have yet to convey to anyone this second 'volte-face' – what a fool they will all think me, but at least people here will in future see through the façade, which must be beneficial all round.

If mine has been a barren love, I do believe that it has had its place in a fruitful process – fruitful for me – fruitful, I even dare think, for you. Even if you deny its usefulness to you, I think, with an uncharacteristic self-confidence, that it might have given you more than you now see.

With love and prayers

David

By the time I received this letter I was on my own in my parents' caravan in the Lakes working on my book in order to get it finished before my job in the bookshop began. The last chapter of my book on the religious life was within hours of completion; it felt crucial to me to have it over and done with, as then the process of coming to terms with it all would be complete – at least for the time being. I had always conceived the project in therapeutic terms, and for that reason had been as honest as I possibly could about my reactions and those of the sisters. Yet I had also refused to minimize the beauty and the allure of the life. For so many reasons, I needed to finish it and draw a line under the whole experience.

Just at this pivotal point, David's letter arrived. His comments on our relationship devastated me; I wanted to crawl away and die. Instead, I forced myself to carry on with my book and finish the last chapter. When it was done, I drove to a nearby hotel overlooking Lake Windermere, and ordered myself a double gin and tonic. I sat on the terrace and drank it as the sun went down over the lake, vowing that from then on I would go it alone.

The next day I went home to Southport; and David rang the Bishop Visitor whose job it was to regulate the community's life. When he discovered that the Bishop was away on holiday and had never received the fateful letter about his resignation which he had sent, David instructed the secretary to burn it, and to say nothing of its contents. He then phoned Frank and Mother Frances to tell them that he had changed his mind yet again, and also informed Dom A, the senior monk who was orchestrating the community's response.

There were guarded reactions all round, except from Poppy, who immediately dashed off a forceful letter on the train from Edinburgh to Oxford. It began: 'At a distance, and several removes, I have been hearing about your gyrations (if that doesn't sound too pejorative a term) and I'm getting concerned.' She argued passionately that David needed to get away from the community, from the effects of institutionalization, if he wanted to make any worthwhile decisions about his future. In a sense it didn't matter *where* he went, as long as he got out – for a minimum of six months. Then, in her view, he would be in a position to sort out his priorities – both about Nashdom and about me – without the pressures that were making him change his mind almost every hour.

With Poppy chivvying them along, events moved rather faster from then on. David spent the weekend of 9–11 September 1983 first at St Gregory's, which had now changed hands, then with James Coutts at Brecon, and finally with Brendan and Morwenna in their new place at St David's. The upshot of his visit was that it was agreed by all that he would spend a sabbatical of three months at St Gregory's with Arthur, who was the new owner, but known to David from previous visits.

Two days after David's return there was the official Chapter, where they were to discuss his resignation. To everybody's relief, he merely asked for three months' leave of absence to consider his future. The day after the Chapter he wrote to me in high good humour, obviously relieved that at least his immediate future was resolved. He apologized profusely both for his letter and his 'childish and unreasonable responses' which he admitted came from a sense of rejection. He also wished me a happy birthday!

Although I received no more letters for some weeks, there was a constant flow from David's pen as he brought his correspondence up to date and informed all the key people – once again – of his current state of mind. He rewrote his letter to the Bishop Visitor, this time in an optimistic tone, informing him about his proposed sabbatical and explaining his ideas and plans for a new, more democratic, community.

On 19 September Frank went to Nashdom for a private retreat, and he and David had a final talk. Then David carried out his last jobs: typed out the rotas for the next three months, handed over the financial and administrative organization to the senior monks, and finished off his packing. He was not due to go to Wales until 14 October, and decided to stay in Oxford for the intervening weeks. He left on 22 September – not with

Frank, who had calls to make elsewhere – but in the official car, driven by one of the younger monks.

David then began three weeks of intensive consultations with Mother Frances, James Coutts, the Bishop of Oxford, former members of the community – and, of course, his family. I met him briefly at the start of this round of consultations, and knew straight away that I was right to be out of it, as I felt only mounting irritation at the self-absorption I felt it betrayed. What exacerbated my reaction (probably unfairly) was the occasion of our meeting, which was Sister Ben's funeral.

She had lived for about eighteen months after her cancer was initially diagnosed as inoperable. During that time, she and I had been able to spend a lot of days together, in addition to the holiday and retreat I described earlier. I had visited her frequently in the novitiate, getting to know the latest group of novices quite well. She maintained her zest for life and her sense of humour right to the end, referring to her cancer light-heartedly as 'the piglets'.

Because it was cancer of the stomach, she had had to have fluid drained from her stomach at frequent intervals, as blockages prevented it from dispersing. Whenever she mentioned 'the piglets', we knew that the pressure was mounting and a hospital visit was imminent. As a result, she grew painfully thin, although she remained fond of a glass of wine and could eat well during her good periods.

I moved back north a month or so before her death, feeling guilty because I knew I just could not face the sights and sounds of her final collapse. Mother Frances rang me after a fortnight to warn me that she was going into the hospice, but I put off going to see her until after my birthday, not realising the urgency. By the next weekend, it was too late. She died in the early hours of 24 September, babbling, like Falstaff, of green fields; Mother Frances was with her.

I remember the night she died waking up from a dream that had been about her with tears in my eyes and words from 'The Dream of Gerontius' on my lips: 'Go forth upon thy journey, Christian soul'. Mother Frances rang me up to tell me the news that morning, but I already knew.

She had died during the community retreat led by James Coutts – a fact which no doubt appealed to her sense of irony.

In the conventual mass that morning he spoke movingly about her, and his address was reproduced on a sheet which was handed out with the order of service at her funeral two days later.

At the funeral, the convent chapel was packed with those who had loved her, from all walks of life, and we sang her favourite hymns, which reduced us all to tears. I remember especially 'Dear Lord and Father of Mankind'. She was so close during the singing of it that I could almost touch her.

Just to finish us all off – or at least me – David assisted with the chalice (Father Vincent, the Chaplain General, was the Celebrant) and Mother Frances administered the wafers. It felt unbearably sad.

Yet afterwards, as I walked to the station with David, we talked not about Ben, but about him: his agonies, his doubts, his uncertainties. His self-absorption made me feel alienated and repulsed, and all I wanted was to get back to the bracing air of the north. Worst of all, though, was the sense of deadness that emanated from David. It was as if everything had been chewed over for so long that there was no substance or flavour left in anything.

I wrote to him when I returned:

30 September 1983

What I want most for you from these three months is a return to your real emotional centre. But I do now finally concede that I cannot cause that to happen in you. And that is rather a devastating admission for a perennial optimist like me, as you know.

I feel totally powerless, because the initiative can only come from you, and if you choose some kind of half-life or passivity, that is your choice. It makes me feel rather cold and frightened.

But, despite all that, the last few days have somehow been coloured with a warmth and a tenderness as I have thought about you. I hope the sensation is telepathic, or empathic, or whatever. Take care of yourself . . .

13

The Healing Valley

For the first time since my days in the film library at Oxfam, I was earning enough money to keep myself afloat; and from 4 October 1983 I was living at my parents' home, so my expenses were minimal. I was also teaching two evening classes, which provided extra money for luxuries.

The job at the bookshop was a very pleasurable experience. Not only was it situated between the two cathedrals, but it was also within spitting distance of the Everyman Theatre – absolutely the throbbing heart of Liverpool! I worked with Anne, who had all the wit and savoir-faire of a native Liverpudlian, not to mention vast experience in running academic bookshops. We shared the morning shift, then I was on my own in the afternoons – which were always quieter.

The contact with the students kept us alert and entertained, and they were kind enough not to bother us with purchases before ten or eleven in the morning, so that we had time to read the papers and relish our coffee! I went to one or two of the student functions at the polytechnic if there was a good band playing, but my attempts at socializing were still painful, so I tended to keep my involvement to a minimum.

Back in Oxford, David had clearly had enough of relationships and was looking forward to the isolation of St Gregory's. His letter of 10 October confessed that, despite intensive 'consultations', he was still undecided about resigning. He seemed emotionally exhausted, and relieved just to be gardening at Frank and Poppy's – though he had been summarily dispatched on arrival to see the latest James Bond film with his niece, in an attempt to kick-start him into life! He showed a polite interest in my job, but admitted that he no longer held out any hope of a joint future for us. Nevertheless, he hoped that we wouldn't lose touch, and reiterated that he did still care.

When he finally arrived – on 14 October – at St Gregory's, David found a small community consisting of himself and three others. Jane had been part of the original group with

Brendan and Morwenna, Joyce was new (though known to David), and Arthur was now the owner, having come in at the tail end of the previous regime. Relationships were complicated, but not strained, and they all gradually settled into a lifestyle that placed a restful emphasis on outdoor work: tending the animals and the smallholding. There were guests booked in to the retreat house, but during this early period David spent quite a lot of time making his gallery room habitable and going to farm auctions.

He enjoyed the unusual mix of monastic structure (regular daily offices) and 'family' life, relishing the conversation as well as the food and drink at meetings, and appreciating small things such as log fires and music. The domestic scale of the place made the routine chores more meaningful, but also made him more aware of his personal loneliness. But on the whole, he was happier than he had been for 20 years, and Nashdom with its hothouse pressures rapidly became unreal, almost incredible to him.

Although his letters were much less frequent, he still had the instinct to write to me and share his feelings and thoughts, and from the middle of October onwards we exchanged letters about every ten days.

He seemed to get on very well with Jane, whom I remembered from my time at St Gregory's as a very shy, sweet person. She was missing Brendan and Morwenna, and not adjusting very happily to Arthur's different style of leadership, but with David's arrival she seemed to settle and come out of her shell. Such small triumphs made David feel more of a human being: someone who could relate outside his role and make a positive contribution to other people's well-being simply by being himself. He found to his pleasure that he could also relate well to a group of young students from Atlantic College who came on a retreat – enjoying the noise and stimulation of their company as much as the quiet routine that returned when they had gone.

The most restful activity for him seemed to be digging in the vegetable garden, but when it was raining – as it often was in late October – he helped with jam making and pickling, or whatever other domestic chores were required. By 16 October, he was beginning to think that it would be nice to settle there permanently, and at a meeting with the other three on the future of St Gregory's three days later, he put into words his desire for a permanent involvement with them. The only caveat at that stage was that he couldn't imagine Nashdom paying to keep him there, and the community depended on a contribution of at least £50 per week from each member.

David was well aware that he would have to go back to Nashdom on 9 December as agreed, but had no idea what effect it would have on him, and whether it would reassert its hold. He kept in close contact with James Coutts, who was only an hour or so away in Brecon, and remained a Guardian of St Gregory's as well as a kind of Lord Protector or Regent for David's vocation.

James had arranged for David and Mother Frances to spend a weekend together at his house in Brecon, planning no doubt to resurrect David's monastic commitment in a new and acceptable form. However, David was dubious. The thought of the three of them together discussing David's future without me made me feel upset, and not a little jealous. I heartily prayed that James's wife Stevie would be a fifth columnist on my behalf, as I still remembered her sympathetic warmth from the day when we had gone straight there to tell them of David's devastating volte-face a year previously.

What I expected Stevie to plead on my behalf, I don't know; it was more a desire to be acknowledged as part of the process of David's transformation and not be forgotten. Feeling this way, I found myself unable to write until I had received some communication from David about the weekend:

25 October 1983

Dear David,

I hope you haven't been worried about the time I have taken to reply to your two last letters. I was just about to reply to the first when I got the second, and I was waiting to see if you rang from James Coutts's house before I got down to the second.

Strange that the thought of the three of you together at James's has rather haunted me – like some kind of unholy alliance! I have felt so much the uninvited guest that it seems incredible not to have been included by the three of you phoning me. What delusions of grandeur! But I can't help but concede that it hurts me to be no longer a part of things. I love Frances and James too as you know, which makes the sense of exclusion harder to bear. But I know this is just a childish response – and inappropriate to boot!

Your last letter filled me with hope – not for myself, as I know there is no hope for me there, but because it cheered me to hear you express some stirrings of happiness and hope and thoughts for the future. If Wales restores you to life I will never allow anyone to make disparaging remarks about the Celtic twilight again.

Oh, be happy! And trust your instincts when they tell you how much more nourishing it is to garden and cook and clean on a family scale, for *real* reasons and *real* people. Take care of yourself and cherish yourself – life is too short for all this agonizing . . .

David's reply to this letter was much warmer than he had been for a long time – partly, I think, because the weekend had clarified his feelings for me, but also because I had agreed to his suggestion that we meet up for the first weekend in December when he had left St Gregory's and had a few days before returning to Nashdom.

James had apparently been his usual inscrutable self over the weekend, seeming unsurprised when David told him on the journey home that the 'chemistry' between David and me remained unchanged. Far from attempting to further his rescue plan, James had merely nodded enigmatically and commented that this was 'significant'. All this David conveyed rather cautiously in his letter of 28 October, not wishing to make it sound as if he took for granted a positive response in me, but wanting to convey his new-found certainties none the less: 'Certainly I do still love you, although it is best that you should continue to think that it is not likely to come to fruition.' At the end of the letter he mentioned that Mother Frances was coming again to Brecon for a final consultation before he left at the end of November, but in his mind he was already moving on to the next stage, and our meeting in

December. He said he was looking forward to it very much, but wanted to make it clear that he didn't feel able to meet my parents after the fiascos of the previous year. Perhaps, he suggested, I could find a suitable place for him to stay. He ended on a tentative note that took absolutely nothing for granted:

> I am very happy at the moment, but the future here seems very insecure, and the future at Nashdom not thinkable. So I am nowhere near a solution. I think of our courses now not so much divergent as parallel . . .
> With all my love

I replied by return:

31 October 1983

My dear . . .

I love you so much more than you assume or I reveal in my behaviour or letters. I love you against reason, circumstance and past evidence – on both our parts. In other words, the 'chemistry' persists in me too, even if I give it no thought at all. My most practical days are still invaded by the most vivid daydreams about you.

So believe and accept that my love is there, and that it has finally learnt to exist without demands, expectations or restrictions. Consequently, when you say 'I am very happy at the moment', I am full of joy: joy that you write and tell me about it, but even more joy that you can feel happy – at last – and just for life's sake.

To be practical, I have spoken to Mum and she suggests that the two of them go away for the first weekend in December and leave us the house. Would you like that? It is a lovely house. I think we could be very relaxed and happy on our own here, and I should like you to see it.

David wrote again on 3 November. It had been wet for several days, saturating the valley, so digging had not been possible. He was inside a lot more, doing domestic jobs, more conscious of the strains in their community life and his own loneliness. It seemed as if the honeymoon period at St Gregory's was over.

3 November 1983

A St Gregory's future seems less possible, also the present seems less idealistic. Yesterday evening at dusk I went for a walk. It was nostalgic for nothing in particular – perhaps nostalgic for life, as I walked past the occasional lit cottage or farm. This evening I went again, but this time with you in the foreground of my mind. The need to walk reflects, perhaps, a new restlessness.

He was clearly very conscious that his 'calm withdrawal into the Welsh hills' was beginning to break up, and everything in him was 'straining forward' to our weekend together in December, regardless of whether or not it was a good thing: 'It will be so very good to see you. I do love you very much, and only hope that that is not too unfair to you. I am sure Rosemary could/does disapprove. I almost do myself.'

Clearly, things were beginning to shift ground in him emotionally, but he was still worried about the effect that 'reimmersion' in Nashdom would have on him. My letter in reply was on a determinedly reassuring note:

9 November 1983

For what my impression is worth, I think your stay at St Gregory's is doing the very warming up that the monks could never facilitate in you – because it is *real life*, ordinary relationships, meaningful tasks, etc. which will do it. I also cherish the conviction that the most direct route to your heart is physical – whether sensual or via your natural/material surroundings.

By the time David replied to this letter, he seemed to have settled down at St Gregory's again and found himself being very open with people about Nashdom and about his enjoyment of life in Wales. This very openness made him feel that things would be very different when he went back to the monastery, if only because of the number of people he had confided in. The length of his absence had also had a severing effect, to the extent that he felt that 'the internal decision' was behind him. In reply to a friendly letter from the Bishop

Visitor, he had written that though he would go back with an open mind, nothing so far made him feel that he would be able to continue as abbot. David also wrote that he was feeling very 'monogamous' because of his feelings for me: '13 November 1983: You are the only person I want to touch and kiss in any way.' He was finding it almost impossible to be demonstrative in the way that came naturally to others, and could not take any kind of touch lightly. The whole thing was too highly charged for him, perhaps because of such long deprivation and self-control. Conscious of how this might raise hopes in me, he also wrote: 'This is not to say that I can love you as you wish to be loved, or that I can get myself together to achieve economic independence.' Yet he added that he was looking forward so much to our meeting in Liverpool that he was afraid he might well be 'tiresomely ecstatic'!

My reply on 20 November was very matter of fact, trying to keep the 'lid on things' in case the meeting in December did not come up to expectations. I told him a lot about recent events – a trip to Norwich to see my sister, Liffy, recent social evenings with friends of the family, plans for helping with a children's party. And there were lots of details about meeting in Liverpool: going to see the shop, perhaps visiting the two cathedrals . . .

David's reply was hopeful, but tentative:

23 November, 1983

> My heart lies with you (or is that romantic nonsense) but I do so fear betraying you again once Nashdom gets its grip on me again . . .
>
> Every day and most of every day I think of you. Of Nashdom I am dimly aware as the place where it must all be thrashed out.

As far as day-to-day living was concerned, he was enjoying himself hacking plaster off the sacristy wall, where he had discovered a large patch of dry rot. His time at St Gregory's was coming to an end, but it had left him in a very positive state of mind to face what was to come: '23 November 1983: Strangely I feel no apprehension – just a great calm.' He left the valley on Monday, 28 November, to go to James's and Stevie's house at Brecon, and he was to leave there the following Friday for Oxford and his brother's house. From there, early on Saturday morning (3 December) he was to travel up to Liverpool for our long-anticipated meeting.

I wrote:

Your last letter had a very strange and lovely effect on me – on reading it I felt suddenly *flooded* with warmth and hope, and the sense of being loved. All the barriers of caution and scepticism came down in a great rush, and I began to believe again in the possibility of a future for us together. It made me realize how long I have lived on starvation rations and pretended to myself that they were enough.

You are so very dear to me, and you complement me so much, in the broad obvious ways, and in such subtle, delightful ways that they are like hidden, erogenous zones. I want so much to be *real* with you, to be more and more myself with you, to stretch and be loved, like an uninhibited cat in front of a warm fire.

And I want exactly the same for you. So even now I cannot see all the horrific bits we have had as wasted – because we have learnt so much about each other, and a lot of it refreshingly bad . . .

I am particularly reassured by the new self-mockery which has begun creeping into your letters. It makes you seem so much more *present*, with your feet solidly on the ground.

How odd to think of these momentous events so near to a conclusion at last . . . I bet you will be sad to leave that lovely valley, and the house itself – and Jane, and the others. I am glad you felt so much at home there; it deserves much gratitude.

Come soon. I cannot wait much longer.

All my love,

H

14
Resolution

Brecon was swallowed up in Liverpool and Southport. In the event, it was hardly alluded to; it seemed to lie in another world that had fallen over the edge of time.

The meeting in Liverpool – at Lime Street Station – was vintage *Brief Encounter*, but there was a kind of reticence, almost awkwardness, between us as I showed David the bookshop, the cathedrals, the theatre bistro, all my favourite haunts. Gradually, I became aware that they were creating a distancing effect as they were not *shared* experiences; and that it would be better to go home to our warm, welcoming house, and shut the door against the world – at least for these two and a half days that were ours alone.

We walked up the hill to Exchange Station and got on the little local train that would take us to Ainsdale, three stops before Southport itself. The house was right opposite the old-fashioned station buildings, and resonated to the comfortable sound of the trains trundling through and the barriers rising and falling at the level crossing.

It was fine, but cold, so one of the first things we did on arrival was to light a log fire – which we resolved to keep burning all weekend as a kind of symbol. This resolution necessitated frequent forays to the nearby beach to collect driftwood – a very acceptable chore. I had always loved the beach in the winter when it was desolate and windswept, and we were able to vary the intensity of our indoor existence with wild struggles against the wind and cold.

I cannot now tell what we did with all the hours and minutes we had together. Sometimes time galloped, sometimes it seemed to dance a slow lyrical minuet, with words and silence woven together and shot through with intense joy. I remember lots of cups of tea, sitting on the rug side by side in front of the fire. There must have been food, but I remember only the wine, and the way it glowed deep red in the firelight. There was also an old film with Bette Davis which we enjoyed together – that much I remember.

How we knit up all the ravelled skeins of months and years of misunderstanding and pain is lost to me. I only remember a

strong, steady flame of physical tenderness and desire –
something that burns in my memory like rapture, something
that was strong enough to hold us together through all the
doubts and uncertainties that were still to come.

David returned to Oxford and his brother's house on Monday
afternoon, 5 December; and quite quickly he revealed to Frank
and Poppy the momentous change that had occurred in him
and his new confidence for the future. Poppy's spontaneous
response was 'Thank God for that!' In his letter the following
day he wrote:

6 December 1983

> I am not going back to Nashdom with an open mind, but with
> a mind made up. This will not make the process less ghastly,
> but at least I shall hope not to be torn inside . . . The weeks
> away from Nashdom were the necessary preparation, but our
> weekend together has given me the confidence to believe that
> you love me enough to forgive all the many ways in which I
> fall short of what I would want to be for your sake.

It was a poignant letter – so full of hope, but so vulnerable
until he had received my reactions to the weekend and knew
them to be the same as his. His letter ended: '6 December 1983:
This comes with all my love, as I begin to try to believe, usually
unsuccessfully, that there could be the joy beyond imagining
of a future together . . . Help me to be worthy of you, David.'
Two priest friends in Oxford independently told him that they
believed both his resignation and his leaving to be not only com-
prehensible, but right. This, together with Frank's and Poppy's
staunch practical support, increased his sense of resolution and
confidence as he faced his imminent return to Nashdom. He
wanted me to know that he regretted his inability to make firm
promises or give me a clear timetable for the future sequence of
events, but he assured me that he would not turn back:

9 December 1983

> . . . do be assured that whatever the wrangles, arguments,
> rows and negotiations, my love for you will not waver . . .

With you I can believe in God's mercy, love, patience and forgiveness; without you I cannot. With you, I can be a person and a priest; without you, I cannot. Not only do I know it, but others perceive it to be true.

The difficulty was going to be in conveying these truths to the monks at Nashdom without making any reference to his love for me. He was determined to omit any mention of me, not only to avoid provoking a scandal (for both our sakes, and theirs as well), but also because there were other reasons for leaving that were fundamentally to do with his life at Nashdom and his relationship with the monks. He wanted to get these over to them in a calm atmosphere that would cause the least damage to all.

By a providential coincidence, the Nashdom car (sent to collect him) had broken down and he was staying on for lunch at Frank's. Consequently he was there to receive my card and letter, which arrived by a late second post. Apparently, they contained all the reassurance he needed on his return. He wrote on 10 December 1983, his first full day back: 'I have your letter and card in their envelope pressed stiffly against my chest in my inside pocket.'

Meanwhile, back in the bookshop, I was taking advantage of an early afternoon lull to write to him again, conscious that he would need something to ward off negative thoughts on his return:

9 December 1983

It is 1.30 pm, and I wonder where you are now – if you have actually got there yet. It is not hard for me to imagine the terrible sinking feeling which must be coming over you if you have got inside and encountered the silence and the queer self-absorbed unreality.

I wonder if you still feel very nervous. What a good thing it was that you felt so nervous because it meant that the issue had become *real* to you. It always chilled me a little on former occasions that you seemed so untouched by it all.

I love you so much that I feel as if my insides have been unbearably stretched to cover the distance between us ('like gold to ayery thinnesse beate') . . . Something has changed so utterly – I seem to have no doubts, only a deep sense of fitness, and a widening sense of the richness we are yet to uncover between us . . .

Next door, in the Students' Union, they have been playing John Lennon songs, and I keep hearing 'Woman', which we had on at the weekend. I can hardly bear to hear it, it is so redolent of the tenderness we shared. . . . This Wednesday night, and all through the next day and night, I found myself haunted by a phrase which was familiar yet unknown, full of poignant associations yet untraceable. It was: 'pay to her usury of long delight'. Eventually I teased out the whole quotation, and recognized it as a verse from Spenser's Marriage Song or 'Epithalamion'. There are a lot of rather wry comments in it by the bridegroom who wants his bride to *get up* and come to the church (!), but the heart of the poem is the bit I remembered:

> For lo the wished day
> Is come at last
> Which shall for all the pain
> And sorrows past
> Pay to her usury of long delight

One day I will show you the whole poem. It is so beautiful. If ever I asked for a wedding present from you it would be an old bound volume containing that one simple poem.

Today, for some reason – on the train into work – my mind allowed itself a little liberty to dwell on the prospect of *our* marriage day. I hardly dared dwell on it; but even there it all felt so different: the prospect of at last making those vows, of at last belonging to you, was so vivid and strong that it blocked out all the rest. But I must clamp down on all that until the time, I know . . .

How odd it must seem to you now – how strangely unreal. But *this is the reality, Nashdom is the shadow*. Be strong. Trust the happiness of the new life that we have.

As long as David was abbot, he was able to phone me privately as there was a phone in his office, but his letters were written more and more frequently in his private cell or bedroom, which was hidden away on the top floor. He wrote that he intended to spend more and more time in his cell, rather than in the office, as one of a series of 'discontinuities', all designed to make the monks realize that things were really changing. He had already stopped writing his journal every day, which he had been keeping without a break for almost a decade as abbot. In his own mind he had also rearranged the seating in the refectory – leaving a gap for his post-abbatial self back among the younger monks (they were seated in order of seniority of profession and he was really quite junior, having been there a mere twenty three years, as one of the monks gleefully pointed out).

All this purposeful activity kept him from thinking too much:

11 December, 1983

this place closes like an icy hand round one's heart, and only the life-line to you makes life and love possible.

The crucial Chapter meeting in which he would give notice of his intention to resign as abbot was scheduled for 15 December 1983. The resignation would probably be formally offered at the January Chapter, but much depended on how he prepared the ground on the 15th. Consequently, a lot of his time between his return to Nashdom and 15 December was spent in individual interviews with the monks. What he wanted to do was concentrate on his own spiritual crises, which would not only arouse sympathy rather than anger, but would also deflect suspicions away from outside influences. It was not spontaneous or cathartic, or even completely honest; and it was not the way I would have done it, but it was the way he had to play it for his own peace of mind:

12 December 1983

It distresses me that I cannot handle it all exactly as you would wish, but much depends on the sort of response I get from the Chapter . . . I do put the consideration of your wishes and feelings first, but I know that I also do this when I act in such a way as to emerge as whole and unscathed as possible. Remorse and a bad conscience are not easy to live with . . .

One of David's 'discontinuities' was to stay away from community recreation, so that he had very little social contact with the monks, except at the private interviews. Offices in chapel and meals in refectory were, of course, silent, except for practical and liturgical communications. He was back into his daily chores, such as feeding the wayfarers and washing up, and he also took a daily walk – partly for exercise, but also to post his letter to me in a public post-box.

His life was so restrained, so circumspect, and I was so free and so impatient to begin our brave new life together, that there was bound to be a conflict of interests. I knew I had to be patient, but there were many passionate phone conversations during December in which I argued for an immediate no-holds-barred presentation of the facts to the monks, and he argued just as forcefully for the merits of taking it slowly and piecemeal. David was convinced that the abbacy and the dispensation of vows had to be taken separately, and that there must be no mention of me.

It wasn't pure selfishness on my part, for I was really afraid that he would revert to his old 'Wilfrid' persona to meet this last crisis, whereas I wanted him to do it from his new, integrated self so that he would come through the fire whole.

What gradually emerged as the way through was something of a compromise. David found as he talked to the individual monks about his spiritual agonies and doubts that they were much more sympathetic than he had dreamed they would be, and he was thus able to tell something like three-quarters of the truth – only stopping short at confessing the existence of our relationship. He wrote:

13 December 1983

> . . . more and more I find I lay emphasis on the crucial factor of increasing unreality throughout my monastic life and not just my abbacy. Thus I feel that I am beginning to meet your point about taking both issues together instead of consecutively. That is to say, I feel that I am presenting the truth of the matter rather than another fabrication contrived to meet the occasion.

He was strengthened in his resolve by letters from other senior church figures that were beginning to come in, offering him support over his proposed resignation and allaying his fears of a scandal in the wider church community. While he inched forward towards the Chapter meeting I was struggling to keep my emotional life from running riot, as the letters testify:

12 December 1983

> This is not going to be a sensible letter. There is so much I want to say, but the feelings are so deep that I can hardly name them to myself, let alone write them in a letter.
>
> I keep seeing flashes of scenes from our future life together, as if they had already happened. And I realise, as you say, that we have hardly begun.
>
> Perhaps I am going off my head! They say deprivation can produce hallucinatory effects. But I love you so much.
>
> Can we have a really adult marriage? One of those that refuses to deceive, mutilate and compromise each other's integrity? Can we meet and trade in freedom? Can we be so honest, so humorous, so indulgent, so stringent and so wildly and skilfully sensual that nobody will be able to touch us for miles?!
>
> Who can stop us? I should like to go to Italy with you for our honeymoon, if you could countenance it. Florence, Venice, Rome for the intellect and the aesthetic sense, and then some remote, deserted sunlit beach (with a large bed) for all the other senses! Oh, my darling, what are all these cold, dark weeks at Nashdom weighed in the balance with what we have to come?

This letter arrived the afternoon before the Chapter at the end of a bad day. One of the younger monks, who had previously been very sympathetic and supportive, had been in to tell David that, after long consideration, he thought it wrong for David to resign. Mother Frances had also dropped in on her way to a speaking engagement to tell him the scandalizing news of a much-respected priest who had left his wife and children and run off with another woman. Both these communications had reinforced his own lurking dread of the scandal and distress his resignation and subsequent marriage could well cause. Thus he was more determined than ever to keep everything separate and avoid any breath of scandal. He wrote:

14 December 1983

Let us so handle the successive stages of this process with love, patience, hope, joy, that we shall feel no shadow from the past . . . Deep down in the knowledge of our love, I feel peace, and from that peace I draw a gentleness, patience and loving concern that shall, I hope, make all things well for all who are involved . . .

On the evening before the Chapter, David tried to phone me, but I was out at a hastily arranged Christmas meal for the bookshop staff and friends – and it was too dangerous to phone Nashdom to let him know. As it was, I was already disguising my handwriting, using typewriters, and posting the letters from different towns. We couldn't risk a direct communication, I well knew, but it was very hard not being able to encourage him before the fateful day.

His letters had reported that the community seemed in good heart, and, if anything, were excited rather than apprehensive about the possibility of change that the crisis presented. The previous abbot, Dom Augustine, had offered to resume the abbacy for the two-year term permitted to him, if David thought the monks would find it acceptable. Everything hung on the decision of the Chapter.

I waited with bated breath in the bookshop, serving the students with a more than usually distracted air, willing everything to be all right. When David finally phoned, it was to say that the meeting had been an anti-climax. He had simply told the monks that a deepening sense of personal crisis made it impossible for him to carry on as abbot, and that he wanted to offer his resignation formally at the next Chapter. A date was set for 4 January 1984 – coincidentally the twenty-fourth anniversary of his arrival at Nashdom. If the resignation went through unopposed, the election for a new abbot would take place later that month. Much depended upon who was elected abbot in David's stead, and how he reacted once he found out about his desire to leave.

15

The Crucial Chapters

Although we were both so wrapped up in these legal processes, Christmas was also approaching, and I was casting around to find a suitable Christmas present for David. In a rather poignant attempt to imagine his new life, perhaps in a parish in Wales, perhaps at St Gregory's, most probably alone – at least in the beginning – he asked for a sleeping-bag. A torch was his only other suggestion!

At home in Ainsdale I was making the Christmas puddings with my mother. I had finished writing my Christmas cards and done most of my present buying – and was in the unfamiliar position of wishing Christmas over, so that 4 January would arrive more quickly.

David's letters continued to be full of the minutiae of community customs and procedures. He explained that if/when his resignation was accepted at the Chapter meeting, the government of the community would pass to the three senior monks. Dom Augustine (who was the most senior) would act as chairman, convener and spokesman up to and including the election Chapter, which would probably be at the end of January.

In response to my desire to see him, he wrote that it would depend on the attitude of the community towards him after his resignation. Would they want him around or would they want him out of the way while they did their electioneering? On a personal note, he described a conversation he had recently had with the same young monk who had previously told him it was wrong to resign. In a renewed salvo, the monk had denounced David's proposed resignation as only another 'no' to life. David commented: '17 December 1983: I did not feel able to say that it is in fact the biggest "yes" to life and love that I have ever made.'

David had also been experiencing Christmas preparations in a family setting – if only at second hand, as he had been for a meal, the night after the Chapter, with some very dear friends who lived nearby. Sally, the mother of two small girls, had been making a dolls' house for her daughters, and David felt drawn into the excitement and warmth as he shared with them his hopes for the future. Both Sally and her husband John (an enthusiastic companion on David's wild flower and butterfly hunts) had connections with Nashdom, and David was very reassured by their understanding and lack of shock at his plans.

Yet the visit intensified his sense of feeling like a child outside in the dark, looking in on the brightly lit scenes of family life. He wrote that he envied me the sheer ordinariness of my Christmas shopping, and I understood exactly what he meant, for I remembered my own feelings in the convent, especially at Christmas. I wrote in my letter of 17 December:

> I knew very well what you meant by 'ordinary' when you described my Christmas shopping. It's the kind of pastime I long to be able to enjoy with you. Our first year should be crammed full of 'lovable ordinariness'. We are peculiarly fitted for experiencing the ordinary with the intensity of children, or even prisoners, finally released . . .
>
> But I am very conscious of the contrast between our two worlds at the moment. Mine is all cosy, commercial, family-orientated, TV-centred – a rich, sentimental Christmas, with a hollow where you should be, and another hollow where Advent should be with its pared-down anticipation of the holy night. Yours – if my experience is anything to go by – will be the complete opposite in every particular, like a garment turned inside out.
>
> There will be the austere beauty of the offices and midnight mass, which may well pierce you, as they will be happening for the last time. But perhaps you too will feel – as I used to – the terrible bleakness of the day itself, with no real family warmth, no spontaneous fun, no excitement from presents and rituals.
>
> I long to have both. And when we are at last together, I dare to hope that it will be so. That the whole of our life together will be sacramental.

He replied on 21 December:

> I think there is a child-like quality in both of us, which I do not think we shall ever lose. I feel that I have no past, only a

future. My past is only significant in bringing me to this point – this unlikely conjunction of David aged 46 and Helen aged 34 – both unmarried, strangely precocious children of the spirit, healed by their wounds.

As Christmas drew inexorably nearer, we exchanged cards and even more letters than usual. I sent him another book (one by Laurens Van der Post, called *Merry Christmas, Mr Lawrence*), and we plotted rather desperately to see if we could make a space to see each other during the festivities. It soon became clear, though, that it wasn't going to work. The only time that he could escape was 27 December – to spend a day with Frank and Poppy in Oxford; and we were having a family party of our own that day in Ainsdale. So it seemed that we would just have to rely on daily phone contact, as before.

David continued to go through his possessions and files in the abbot's office, removing or destroying anything personal, withdrawing himself more and more from the exercise of abbatial authority. His plan at this stage was to negotiate a parish for himself in the Swansea and Brecon diocese, where he would be near James Coutts and St Gregory's, but be able to function in his own place. He seemed to want to be alone for the early months of 1984 and 'win his spurs' before I joined him.

The question of how to arrange all this, and circumvent the difficulties, now exercised his mind. There seemed very little problem from the parish angle – as the Bishop of Swansea and Brecon had been making positive noises. However, David didn't yet know if the Chapter would accept his resignation; he knew that he could insist upon it, after consulting the Bishop Visitor, but there was the additional problem of whose authority he would be under between resignation and dispensation of vows, and how they would react to his plans. The latter issue suddenly took on real urgency when Dom Augustine made it clear to David that he might have to get permission from the triumvirate to have leave of absence for any length of time after his resignation.

Long experience on the Advisory Council for Religious Communities had taught David a ruse or two, so he knew that the best course was to seek 'exclaustration' from the next abbot, which would put him under the authority of a bishop until he could be released from his vows. If he was to be in a Welsh diocese, this would work perfectly. He did not use this knowledge, but simply persuaded Dom Augustine to agree to his absence in the short term. He was quite clear that he didn't want to be around on the evening of his resignation Chapter, so he had arranged to have dinner on the night of 4 January with Sally and John again. After that, he was to go to Oxford; and unbeknown to both Oxford and Nashdom, he intended to travel up to Ainsdale to spend the weekend of Epiphany with me: 'So that is Friday January 6th' he wrote, 'the day when wise men follow their star'.

My mother and father were going away for a long, post-retirement holiday in Spain the week after Epiphany, and David and I had agreed that it would be good to see them before they went, so that they knew how things stood. It would also be our true celebration of Christmas, as we could celebrate his liberation from twenty-four years of exile. I wrote to him on St Thomas's Day:

21 December 1983

Christmas has suddenly filled out and lost the bleakness at its heart since you have revealed to me the *real* date of the feast. I had felt so bad about the prospect of going back to work without your ever being made a real physical part of the celebrations. Now everything feels solid and real.

There may be a little reserve on Mum's and Dad's part, but it will be easily overcome when they see the change in you (and indeed in me, when you are there) – and, anyway, the resignation itself will have so changed matters that one cannot predict anything with accuracy.

It was because of this inability to predict anything with accuracy that we both experienced a mounting sense of strain as first Christmas approached and then 4 January. The image that appeared to sustain David at this time was the prospect of the two of us in a simple country cottage, out in the garden, or making food together, with no more excitement needed than a trip into town to look around a secondhand bookshop or visit an auction to pick up some furniture. The image was transferable from Wales to Lancashire or Cumbria as far as he was concerned – if that would make things easier for me. His only anxiety was that I should be content and not feel trapped.

He had a meeting with the Bishop Visitor. It was interesting that the Visitor did not press David to change his mind, quite the opposite in fact. His comment when he saw David was that he looked what his wife would call 'dans le vrai' ('in the truth'), and, that he had been absorbing the community's negativity for too long.

This was a great load off David's mind and made it possible for him to face the ordeal of Christmas with some degree of equanimity.

It wasn't the liturgical acts which were so daunting. Hearing confessions, celebrating the midnight mass left him with a sense of rightness that this phase was coming to an end and something new about to begin. The contact with visitors also provided a kind of balm as they said such positive things to him about the way he had changed. One friend even commented that his voice had changed, as she said goodbye after midnight mass:

25 December, 1983

> Of course you have changed, changed completely, even your voice is different. It comes from here (indicating stomach) and not from here (indicating throat), and people even dare to stand and talk with you.

The really daunting thing was to sit through all the community meals and corporate celebrations, as if nothing had changed, and he had no intention of betraying them. His role was to be father to the monks; part of him, at least, felt like Judas.

We had a long emotional phone conversation about this on Christmas night, giving each other strength to hold out the remaining ten days. I didn't get his phone call on Boxing Day evening, though, because the family had gone to my brother's for a celebratory meal, and though I had dashed back across Southport, I had not got back in time before the Greater Silence descended at Nashdom and a ringing telephone would be too conspicuous.

Such accidents of traffic and timing dogged our communications over the Bank Holiday, until at last the mail began to get through again on Wednesday, 28 December.

In his first letter after the holiday period, David described his feelings as he unpacked his annual Christmas present from two of the oblates, a desk diary for 1984:

28 December 1983

As I looked at its blank pages I could not but reflect that probably the most momentous year in my life will eventually be recorded within its covers. Never have I confronted a year with so few fixed points in it.

I have in fact broken the consistent practice of nine years and written nothing in this year's diary since 9 December. Partly this has been one of my deliberate discontinuities, but mostly it has been a very private time when all my significant living has been done on a level which I have no wish to record there.

I must now decide how to use the 1984 diary, which I want to start on January 1st. Or, should I wait, I wonder, until the 4th?

The post had also brought a card that had touched him deeply:

28 December 1983

Someone who has no reason to think there is any joy or hope in my life has sent a card which has these words upon it: 'For lo, the winter is past, the rain is over and gone. The flowers appear on the earth, the time of singing has come, and the voice of the turtle dove is heard in our land.' It is a quotation from the Song of Songs, which I am sure you know, and begins with the line 'Arise, my love, my fair one, and come away'. The whole passage really says everything that needs to be said! You might read it through, before I find it necessary to quote it all!

I had in fact read it through many times and recited it to myself as a kind of talisman, not only in the difficult times with David, but in my most hopeless days in the convent. Neither of us, at this stage, quite dared to claim it for our own. I wrote to David daily amid the protracted family celebrations, amazed by my own sense of disjunction when I was usually so happy to be with them all:

I have been in a strange state these last two days, unable to simulate the festive spirit at all. The social trigger doesn't seem to work. I find myself suddenly 'waking up' in situations where I should have been scintillating or at least listening, and I haven't been present at all. I feel half-alive, like somebody on starvation rations, who has to move very slowly because her pulse is barely beating.

I didn't expect to feel like this: the ferocity of the sense of loss, of waste of days, and of sheer absence has really caught me off balance. I feel it in physical symptoms of breathlessness, incredible tension, inability to swallow without conscious effort, and this pervading sense of limbo. I suppose this must be love!!

On 30 December, five days before the Chapter, David wrote:

30 December 1983

I would incidentally make it quite clear that I shall leave without the slightest tinge of regret or sadness. To leave in any case would be a vast relief. To leave for a future with you is a joyous prospect beyond words. I have never enjoyed life here, never felt at home; 'David' has always stood on the outside, shackled to the place, but never consenting. He is a difficult and stubborn character, you will perceive. What is more, he finally got his way – only with your help, of course. The ultimate pertinacity was not about staying after all, but about leaving.

As the year drew to a close, some of the monks began to express great anxiety, as a result of all the waiting and the uncertainty. One of the senior brethren tried to persuade David to stay on after his resignation in order to ensure a smooth transition. Yet despite lingering qualms about his duty to the monks, David was at last able to take a firm line and say that they would have to manage things without him. The prospect of being around while the community picked up the pieces and started again was unbearable to him and would have been undignified for the community.

One of the younger monks, who was almost the same age as David, took a rather more prophetic line and came in to share with him his discovery about Jung's theory of 'creative disasters', making it clear that he himself felt that 'disaster' would provide the necessary way forward for them all.

Abbot Benedict, from Nashdom's daughter community in America, sent a letter on New Year's Day written in direct personal terms, advising David to find someone to share his inner thoughts and feelings over the next months as he would undoubtedly experience grief at the loss of his abbatial role. His letter ended with these words: 'So for this new year journey . . . blessings. Jesus can go wherever you need to go. Affectionately, Benedict.'

During the last few days of 1983, he wrote 28 letters, tying up all the loose ends, informing all the necessary people. His files were all in order; his private possessions removed from the abbot's office. He wrote that he was feeling 'tense, but not strained'. It was as if he was emerging into an open space.

The morning of the 4th, he had a communication from the 'real world' which particularly heartened him – a letter of support from one of his oldest childhood friends. It was like a dispatch arriving on the field of battle just before hostilities commenced.

It was a brilliant, clear day, and he felt very calm. He had woken up early after his first wedding dream, which he took to be a good omen. It was 24 years to the day since he had come as a postulant.

His resignation was typed out and ready, and he spent the time before the Chapter sorting out the details of how its presentation should be handled.

On the afternoon of 4 January 1984 he read out the following statement:

RESIGNATION OF ABBACY

I hereby place my resignation before the Chapter on this 4th day of January 1984, in the tenth year of my abbacy.

It is not necessary here to analyse the causes that have brought me to this decision; it is enough to consider their effects.

1. The community has been in a state of uncertainty for more than two years while I have grappled with the resignation issue.
2. This has been the culmination of a longer period during which I have found myself increasingly unable to fulfil effectively the responsibilities of abbacy.
3. I now find myself incapable of facing, and certainly not handling, important questions that now confront the Chapter.

In 1982 I felt, in the event, that I could and should continue in office. This time I believe that I cannot and should not do so.

I am not asking the Chapter to approve my resignation, only that they accept it.

My sole anxiety is that my resignation might encourage negative reactions at a time when a spirit of discernment and much good will and mutual understanding are most necessary.

4 January 1984

Dom Wilfrid Weston, OSB
Abbot

The statement was received in complete silence.

That evening – as planned – was spent at his friends who lived a stone's throw from Nashdom. His last private phone call from the abbot's office conveyed the news to me. I responded with a card containing some of my favourite lines from *Antony and Cleopatra*, in an attempt to convey the intensity of my feelings: 'Lord of Lords! O infinite virtue, comest thou smiling from the world's great snare uncaught?'

Our Epiphany was a mixture of ecstasy and exhaustion, in which exhaustion predominated. We both felt rather flat – I because he was out and yet still not free, he because he was too dazed to grasp that he was out, disorientated by a world without boundaries and deadlines. I then returned to work, and

David returned to his brother's house where the family provided a base for him to pursue his consultations with various bishops about a job.

The Bishop of Leicester, Visitor to the community, and the Bishop of Oxford both gave him their support with great delicacy and tact as he pursued these enquiries; but it wasn't until he had had a positive response from the Bishop of Swansea and Brecon (whom he had visited on the day after his weekend with me) that I realized how afraid he had been of rejection from the church hierarchy. When Frank was also able to assure him of the support and sympathy of the other Oxford bishops and archdeacons, he seemed released to follow up the possibility of jobs in the Church of England, and particularly in the north.

Two days after my return to work and his interview with the Bishop of Swansea and Brecon, I had an interview with the Bolton Institute of Higher Education, where it would be possible, if accepted, for me to do a Postgraduate Certificate in Education, specializing in further and higher education. It seemed a sensible use of my degree, and an insurance against the precariousness of the Liverpool job. Suddenly everything seemed to be pointing towards the north, and David was relieved to have his options reduced – though fearful of his desire to accept whatever was offered in order to please me.

We were both romantic enough to have dreams about an idyllic country vicarage where we could just potter about and be ourselves, but there wasn't much wild countryside between Southport and Bolton, so we knew that realism would have to prevail.

David wrote to my parents after the Epiphany weekend, thanking them for their sympathy and understanding and assuring them that he hoped to have a job arranged by the time they returned from Spain at the end of March. To my relief, he acknowledged his responsibility for the disappointments of the past and expressed his conviction that things would be different this time:

10 January 1984

I do assure you that Helen's happiness is my primary concern, and I shall do everything in my power to secure this.

I am painfully conscious of what happened in 1982, but I do feel that both for Helen and myself the circumstances are now entirely different and altogether more positive and encouraging.

He also reassured them that we would do nothing precipitate about marriage plans while they were away.

Yet my parents were not the only sceptics he had to face. When I drove them down to Heathrow on the weekend of 14 January, I stayed with Rosemary, who suddenly erupted with all her misgivings about David's volte-face after the 'betrayal' of 1982. Her reaction was triggered by answering the phone to him while I was at her house, and suffering from his notoriously brusque telephone manner.

David was unable to be there in person to talk things over with her, as he had suddenly been summoned to hospital for a wisdom tooth extraction. He was, however, anxious to restore good relations with her, and asked me in his letter to try and explain how strong Nashdom's hold on him had been at that time, so that it was not lack of love, but lack of belief in himself, that had made him turn his back on a future with me.

I was feeling in need of reassurance myself at this stage, as a conversation with Mother Frances during the weekend had confirmed me in my belief that David should come clean about his relationship with me before he finally left Nashdom. My motives were mixed, I knew: part of me felt that the monks shouldn't be fobbed off with a half-truth, the other, more selfish part of me, wanted him to acknowledge his love for me publicly, whatever the cost. It was an old argument, but it was becoming more urgent, exacerbated by my desire to have things resolved and his desire to keep resignation and dispensation separate by several weeks, if not months.

David wrote on 15 January 1984: 'Open discussion with the community of my situation is a good idea in principle, and I will take the opportunity if it offers, but one does have to be realistic about what is possible in the monastic situation . . .' He seemed to think that a lot depended on how the Visitor viewed it all, when he came to give his 'charge' to the community on 18 January. If he thought it cathartic for them all to open up such basic issues, then that would change matters considerably.

David was still in hospital when the Visitor arrived, but he had already had an interview with Dom Augustine before going to hospital on 15 January to tell him of his decision to seek dispensation from his vows. He had expected great remonstrations from the ex-abbot, but had received none. The matter would be raised with the Bishop in David's absence.

Two of the monks who were closest to David came to visit him on the day of his operation and advised him not to return to Nashdom for a day or two once he had recovered, but to go back to Oxford and allow things to take their course. On Wednesday, 18 January, the Bishop Visitor delivered his charge to the community with an astringent honesty that nevertheless found room for tenderness. He made no bones about the spiritual devastation that he saw around him, but offered a cautious way forward if the monks were prepared to open themselves up to the healing process and to allow the wound to be cauterized.

It was a plea from the heart that broke down the barriers and made it possible for David also to make himself vulnerable. On 25 January, several weeks before he had anticipated it would be possible, he returned to Nashdom to make his formal application for dispensation from his vows before the assembled Chapter. Again he read out his statement; again it was received in silence. Yet this time it was a full and complete statement, expressing the reasons of the heart as well as of the mind:

Nashdom Abbey
25 January 1984

APPLICATION FOR DISPENSATION OF VOWS

1. I hereby make my application for the dispensation of my solemn vows, taken 20 years ago at Nashdom on 29 June 1964.
2. In setting out my reasons for this, I am not only fulfilling the requirements of the process, but acknowledging that I owe it to many to express myself as truthfully and clearly as possible.

3. Believing myself called by God, I entered the Nashdom novitiate on 4 January 1960. My shyness and withdrawal in fact concealed a deep-seated self-rejection and sense of failure, rooted in experiences of my childhood and upbringing. To a degree that no one could then realize, my response to vocation was in part saying 'no' to life, although by no means without more positive aspects.

4. Determined to make this vocation work, I passed through the stages of the novitiate with few outward signs of difficulty. In my self-doubt I felt that a life that seemed only to require determination and perseverance for success was one that best suited me.

5. At the age of 26, very immature for my years, I made life vows. My novitiate had been passed in the pre-Vatican II mood of spiritual confidence, largely untouched by insights into the complexity of human development.

6. The subsequent years saw considerable progress in my outward life. I passed an ACCM board, did my theological studies and passed GOE. I was given increasing responsibility in the community, and ordination brought with it the new feature of contacts outside the community. My appointment as novice master in 1969, while substantially reducing these contacts which might have assisted emotional development, did nevertheless make me responsible for the first time for the lives of others.

7. By this time, the post-Vatican II era had arrived for the community. While responding to this in my work and on superficial levels of my thinking, deep down I remained locked in a world circumscribed by concepts of determination and perseverance, responsibility and duty. While seeming to achieve a measure of success in my work, inside I remained lifeless and dry in ways that could be accounted for in traditional spiritual terms, but which in fact characterized a life bereft of any real sense of faith, hope and love, or any concept of God's grace, acceptance and forgiveness.

8. So this dual life continued. On the one hand, I was appointed prior in 1971 and abbot in 1974, labouring to make a success of it, and seeming to fulfil monastic

expectations. On the other hand, I knew and accepted that Christian and monastic life for me was not a redemptive process, with stark consequences for my own understanding of God and of my relation to him.

9. This situation which seemed so immutable was radically changed by two events in 1979 and 1980, when I was 41 and 42 respectively. The first event was my mother's death after a short illness (my father had died two weeks after I was born), and the consequent break-up of the place I still thought of as home. This seemed radically to shake the foundations of my life, and to call in question much that I had accepted without reflection. The second event, a year later, was meeting a person who challenged my self-evaluation and the inevitability of my being trapped in a situation seemingly devoid of every redemptive quality, as far as I was concerned.

10. The person concerned was a woman religious in junior vows who was painfully concluding that she should not proceed to life vows. She discussed this with me, and while seeking to help her I unwittingly revealed my exceedingly negative attitude to my own vocation. She left her community soon afterwards, but we kept in touch. She continued to represent to me that monastic vocation ought to stand for positive qualities that should be life-giving rather than life-denying.

11. To me it was a revelation that grace and forgiveness, love and joy might be lived experiences and not just intellectual concepts. All my early responses to this were that this might be true of others, but not of myself. Over the next three years we kept in touch mainly by letter, but also meeting as opportunity offered. It was for me a time of increasing bewilderment and pain as on the one hand I began to grasp something of what she meant, but on the other hand realized how incapable I was of incorporating such insights into my monastic life. All my monastic preconceptions had been fixed in the pre-Vatican II attitudes of my early years, and I found myself quite incapable of changing them. On the other hand, my commitment to my vows and to the promises of my blessing as abbot allowed me no alternative. My

bid to resign as abbot in 1982 foundered on my own inability to see how such a course of action could be justified.

12. Two developments in 1983 resolved this seemingly insoluble dilemma. First there was increasing evidence of disaffection in the community which made me realize for the first time that my negative attitudes were not without their impact on the community, and that my continuing in office was not necessarily in its best interests. Second, the sheer build-up of inner stress brought me to the point where I had to go away for a while to avoid a complete breakdown, torn as I was between feeling that I must continue and feeling incapable of doing so. The consequence of my two-and-a-half-month absence, spent largely in a small community in Wales, was that my reactions shifted from an exclusively cerebral balancing of arguments, to one where feeling had at last broken through to reveal aspects of myself with which I had not previously been consciously in touch. I now simply knew that I could not continue as abbot, and that for me monastic life was inextricably confused with life-denying attitudes which I recognized as being not only negative, but destructive for myself and for others.

13. What I began to perceive was that God who had called me into a life which I was predisposed to believe was all about duty, was in fact calling me again to receive his gift of life in a way that only now was I able to accept it. The destruction of my false preconceptions was the precondition of a new start in a new context, where I could receive day by day the help that I now knew myself to need.

14. This radical solution, I came to see, involved not only my resignation, but the dispensation of my vows to release me from a situation which although potentially redemptive, had been so misinterpreted by me as to defeat its true ends. I recognize that the solution creates new difficulties not only for myself, but for the community and for some outside it. For this I am sorry, but as I have found new life in facing up to the truth about myself, in admitting defeat, in seeing apparent

achievement destroyed, so I believe that ultimately only good can come out of a situation where facing the truth with humility is seen as the best way of knowing God's will.

15. It is my hope, when I have left, to become a parish priest and to marry that person who first represented to me new hope where there had been none. This will, I know, cause offence to some, but I have come, not without initial reluctance and considerable inner turmoil, to recognize its rightness for me, accepting it as a new course to God given by him to one who had thought himself irretrievably lost. In the light of this new hope, I dare to believe that good can come out of this for others also.

25 January 1984   Wilfrid Weston

One of the older monks in the community, whom David regarded as a good and holy man, wrote on 1 February 1984: 'I was deeply moved by your account of how you came to your decision and we must all have been moved.' The Bishop of Oxford, to whom David sent a copy of the statement, wrote on 28 January: 'That must have been hard to write (but it is well done) and even harder to have read out in public, but if a general catharsis has taken place in the community as a result, thank God and take heart.'

By the next day, David had left Nashdom for good, and by the afternoon of the 26th he had phoned the Bishop of Blackburn to request an interview. The Bishop Visitor and David's brother were left to deal with the rapaciousness of the press, while David went up to his Lancashire retreat and tried to adjust his sights to parochial life.

The news did not break officially until the community issued its formal statement on the resignation and impending secularization. The *Church Times* carried it as front page news on Friday, 24 February 1984, by which time David had begun the third day of his new life: as assistant curate in the parish of St Peter's, Chorley.

16

The Winter is Past

Perhaps strangely, we did not take it for granted that David would come and live with me in my parents' house for the period between his departure from Nashdom and the start of his new job in Chorley. Some people would have grasped the opportunity and lived together in the fullest sense, rejoicing in their long-awaited freedom, but it did not seem right for us.

In the end, although we did share a house for a month, it was rather a tentative, complicated time. David was technically still a monk (his dispensation did not reach him until he had started at Chorley, arriving in the post on 28 February 1984), and he was about to become a curate in a traditional Lancashire parish. We had waited nearly three years already. So, although it was a consummation devoutly to be wished, there was at first a tacit, and then an open agreement between us that we would wait a little longer until after the wedding.

We wanted to be married in the sunshine and we wanted to be married somewhere in Oxford, which held meaning and associations for both of us. Ainsdale had no ties for me, and most of our friends lived in or around Oxford, so when Frank and Poppy offered their house in Tom Quad, Christ Church, for the reception, it seemed to confirm our choice.

The tiny, Romanesque church in Iffley village, on the outskirts of Oxford, was very dear to me, both from university days when friends and I used to walk to it down the towpath, and from convent days when I used to spend long silent retreat days on my own there. David was very fond of it too, and the vicar generously gave his permission for us to be married there, on presentation of a special licence (as neither of us was living in the parish). James Coutts was to officiate.

We were feeling very satisfied with the progress of our plans until my parents returned home from Spain, and we realized – belatedly – that we had usurped their role. In taking the organization of the reception out of their hands, and deciding to have it at Christ Church, however perfect the setting might be, we had made them redundant. We tried to make up for this insensitivity on our part as preparations advanced, but the damage was never completely undone, despite goodwill on all sides.

Meanwhile, David and I were trying to make a home for him in the flat that the church had provided in Chorley – above a newsagent, and between a pub and a betting shop! The sleeping-bag that he had asked for as a Christmas present now came into its own, as it was all that he had to his name when he arrived by bus on 21 February. The situation was, however, soon remedied by the resourcefulness and generosity of the vicar and his wife, Carl and Anne Berryman, who immediately adopted him as another member of their expansive and expanding family. Armchairs, a Z-bed, a fridge, a cooker, wardrobes, even carpets, all appeared from nowhere at various times of the day or night. I filled what gaps I could, making almost daily trips over from Ainsdale in my black 1300, feeling like a member of the Swiss Family Robinson, foraging for anything useful in the mother ship!

In some strange way, I was grateful to be able to share the responsibility for David's emotional and spiritual welfare with someone else, and particularly with such seasoned travellers as the Berrymans. It had been surprisingly difficult to come home from a day's work at the bookshop and find David almost completely dependent on me for his contact with the outside world. He had done some heroic gardening – laying out the new garden for my parents on their return – but it was an essentially solitary task. At Chorley, however strange and new it was, he was with friends – and could order his own life.

He preferred to have no contact with Nashdom, although there were occasional, very sweet letters from Dom Godfrey, who was eventually chosen to be abbot (for a two-year period). The community had been three months without a superior – difficult, painful months, by all accounts. Dom Francis kept David up to date with developments, but David's instinct was to keep himself apart.

There was, however, the problem of money. As things stood, we had nothing at all, except our meagre salaries. David decided he would have to write to the community and broach the matter of the money his mother had left to them on her death. It was David's share of the sale of her house, and although technically he had no right to it, he knew that she had meant it for him. But would the community see it that way? So far, they had given him £200 to start his new life.

To their credit they responded with alacrity to his letter, and refunded the money in full, by way of a cheque sent to Chorley on 25 March, the Feast of the Annunciation. It was not a vast amount, but it meant that we were able to put something in the bank as well as buy our own furniture. Our first and greatest acquisition was a hand-carved antique French bed, which we bought from a shop in Southport and had delivered with great ceremony (and some difficulty!) up our narrow outside staircase. We even hired a van in Chorley and drove all the way down to the Cotswolds in it because we had seen some old pine furniture we liked in a village there by the unlikely name of Wyre Piddle. We bought a dresser, a chest of drawers and a bookcase there, as well as another bookcase and a corner cupboard from the indoor market in Oxford, and returned rejoicing with our booty up the M6 to Chorley. Thus we passed the weeks and months until the wished day should come at last.

On 9 June 1984, at 11.30 a.m., (or possibly 11.40 a.m.) it was too late to turn back. The anonymous black taxi drew up at Iffley Church, and my father and I walked down the path to the West Door, arm in arm. No photographers were present, though a friend had stayed outside with his camera to record the moment. The temperature was already in the eighties, and there was a cloudless blue sky.

The bride wore cream – a calf-length dress from a local chain store, with matching shoes. No frills; no train; a vestigial veil on a cream pill-box hat; a small bouquet of cream and yellow freesias. Her father was proud and emotional in grey morning dress. Her sister – the only bridesmaid – was vibrant and quintessentially herself in a red and black chequered cotton suit, with black plimsolls and a bunch of scarlet roses.

We entered the church in a small procession, as the organ played the opening bars of 'Nimrod' – music guaranteed to bring an instant lump to the throat. The church seemed dark and jewel-like after the bright sunlight outside. The aisle was short, and the pews crammed with a blur of smiling faces.

Two black tail-coated figures were waiting at the chancel steps. The slighter of the two turned to reveal an elegant winged collar and grey cravat, held in place by a pearl tie pin. It was a dear, familiar face, but also foreign and strange in this company of friends and relations. James Coutts was there to receive us and bless us 'with his two happy hands', enclosing us at last in the harbour of his arms. There was a profound sense of homecoming.

The first hymn with its Gaelic melody was felt rather than sung, and then the introductory words were upon us:

Marriage is given that husband and wife may comfort and help each other . . . in need and in plenty . . . with delight and tenderness . . . bodily union . . . children . . . reverently, responsibly, and after serious thought . . .

The gravity of the approaching contract was laid upon us and we felt its weight. Then, at last, the cherished words from the Songs of Songs were released into the air, like the dove from the ark: 'Arise, my love, my fair one, and come away. For lo, the winter is past, the rain is over and gone . . .' The flinty passion of Wendy's voice carried the memory of winter in it as well as the joy of the spring, and the hymn that followed took up this theme:

Now the green blade riseth from the buried grain,
Wheat that in the dark earth many days has lain;
Loves lives again, that with the dead has been:
    Love is come again,
    Like wheat that springeth green.

As we sang the words, I felt again how much they belonged to this complex man beside me, how much they described his personal odyssey through the dark lands.

Then it was St John exhorting us to love one another, followed by the sermon. We sat side by side on our dual thrones as James spoke to us in passionate mystical terms of the New Adam and the New Eve, of placing crowns on our heads and joining us in the sacred dance. I remember a sense of perfect fitness about his words, though they floated through my head like dust-motes in sunlight, and were never completely grasped by my rational mind. I was lost in a haze of intense joy, surrounded by all the people I cared about most in the world, on the doorstep of paradise.

The marriage vows, when they came, were like a dash of cold water. Suddenly we were making serious promises. I had been brought up to keep my promises. There was an audible pause after the first question – 'Will you take David to be your husband?' – while I panicked. I felt as if I wanted to read the small print! For what seemed like several minutes, I watched myself like somebody in a film. Then the affirmative words came out of my mouth, and the decision was made. From then on, I began to enjoy myself and was ready to commit myself to loving and cherishing, honouring and sharing – though not 'obeying', not after the long years of obedience in the convent.

We had moved up to the altar as the service progressed to the communion part, and we now knelt before Frank, who presided over the bread and wine with gentleness and warmth. It was moving to see all the people we loved coming up together in a great groundswell to the altar – all the individual faces forming part of the pattern. Everything seemed charged with significance. The words of the hymns and the sermon and the readings wove themselves into the same complex pattern, and for once the pattern was visible.

We stood for the last hymn, 'The Lord of the Dance'. Our journey back down the aisle was bathed in the opulent colours of the rose window, and we burst out of the dark cave of the church into a new and shining world. The congregation streamed out behind us and spread over the grass in a multi-coloured phalanx.

There was just one jarring note: the uninvited presence of a reporter and photographer from the *Oxford Mail*, but they quickly left. There followed much talking, and milling around, and a few photographs taken by friends and family, then the whole company of some 65 souls wound its way down the hill, over immaculate Iffley lock, and into the waiting barge, suitably provided with burnished thrones.

A stately procession down the Thames/Isis followed – James Coutts's idea, as it seemed the most romantic method possible of getting from the church to the house! We moored at Christ Church Meadow (a privilege secured by relations in high places) and promenaded gaily down the broad avenue of trees that leads to the meadow gate of Christ Church.

It must have been quite a sight – such a dazzling and eccentric procession wending its way through the Meadow, and then through the cloisters and quadrangles of Christ Church. We arrived at the imposing door of the archdeacon's lodging, paused for a photograph or two, and then gathered our forces for the final push through the panelled rooms and out into the dappled sunlight of the walled garden.

It was a perfect June day and very hot, but the small tables were all well shaded by trees, with a venerable decaying mulberry forming a canopy in the centre. The French chef of Christ Church, who had generously given his services free, had done such elaborate and wonderful things to the salmon and beef, displayed on a long trestle table with the other food, that we were loth to begin! But hunger triumphed and the celebrations got under way.

I remember tasting most things, but never really eating anything, as I moved from table to table with David, trying to talk to everybody. But I do remember Poppy's crême brulée – as it was my first experience of this ambrosial pudding, and it seemed to symbolize the sensuous perfection of the day.

I must have kissed all 65 guests (David rather less, though a lot for him) at the end of a memorable afternoon, before the garden was left behind and we were driven to the station by my father. I forgot my make-up bag, and my mother didn't realize we were leaving, and consequently missed saying goodbye, but otherwise we escaped most mishaps – including the customary toilet rolls and tin cans tied to the car!

Crispian, David's best man and Poppy's brother, had secretly deposited some champagne in our luggage for our first night, which we spent in a hotel near the airport, before flying to Venice and the Italian Lakes. We were so tired that we fell asleep with the champagne in our hands.

Rosemary, Wendy, James Coutts and Mother Frances – all key players in the drama – dispersed to their own homes and their own lives. Relations and friends from our past and present exchanged names, perhaps even addresses, and parted again for another ten years.

We were left with small icons of memory – the church, the riverboat, the garden – and a sense that our real life was just beginning.

Epilogue

In the years since our marriage, we have moved three times. The first move was for David to become Vicar of Pilling, in Lancashire: a very happy period, during which time our first son, Luke, was born (1986).

In 1989 we moved to the Borders, as David was appointed domestic chaplain to the Bishop of Carlisle. We lived in one end of the bishop's residence which is called Rose Castle. Our second son, Alexander, was born there in 1990.

In 1994 David was made Canon Warden of Carlisle Cathedral and we moved to the cathedral close, where we now live. My own work is chiefly running courses in writing and self-development for women. I also do some counselling. Both David and I have managed to fit in some further study since we married. He now has a doctorate in church history and I have an MA in feminist theology.

The years have proved David right in his conviction that the process of leaving had to be taken slowly and thoroughly. He has hardly ever experienced regret or doubt about the rightness of his decision – only a growing sense of living 'dans de vrai'.

David's community has undergone considerable change since his departure – not least in its move to a new abbey in Speen, Berkshire. The present abbot went out of his way to visit us in Pilling and to reassure David that his leaving had brought benefits as well as pain. It had freed them to reassess the traditional ways of relating and to develop more personal and caring patterns of community life.

So we are left with the more or less abiding sense that 'nothing is wasted' – a pronouncement I first delivered in my sleep to an astounded Rosemary, in the early days after the exodus.